REVISE EDEXCEL GCSE (9–1)
Combined Science

PRACTICE PAPERS Plus⁺
Higher

Series Consultant: Harry Smith

Authors: Stephen Hoare, Nigel Saunders, Catherine Wilson, Allison Court and Alasdair Shaw

---

These Practice Papers are designed to complement your revision and to help prepare you for the exams. They do not include all the content and skills needed for the complete course and have been written to help you practise what you have learned. They may not be representative of a real exam paper. Remember that the official Pearson specification and associated assessment guidance materials are the only authoritative source of information and should always be referred to for definitive guidance.

For further information, go to
quals.pearson.com/gcsesciencesupport

Contents

About this book

The practice papers in this book are designed to help you prepare for your Edexcel GCSE Combined Science examinations. In the margin of each paper you will find:

- **links** to relevant pages in the Pearson Revise Edexcel Combined Science (9–1) Revision Guide
- **hints** to get you started on tricky questions, or to help you avoid common pitfalls
- **maths skills** and **practical skills** hints to highlight questions that cover these skills
- key formulae or definitions that you should **learn** for your exam
- **explore** boxes to help you think about a particular question or topic.

If you want to tackle a paper under exam conditions, you could cover up the hints in the margin.

There are also answers to all the questions at the back of the book, together with information about how marks are allocated. Note that in your examinations, your answers to **6-mark questions** will be marked on how well you present and organise your response, and not just on the scientific content. Your responses should make sure that you show how the points link to each other, and you should structure your response in a clear and logical way.

About the papers

Each paper has **60 marks**. In your exam you will have **1 hour and 10 minutes** to complete each paper, and it will be worth $\frac{1}{6}$ of your qualification. When you sit your examinations you should:

- Use a black ink or ball-point pen, calculator and a ruler.
- Read every question carefully and answer **all** the questions in the space provided.
- Make sure you have shown all your working out – there may be more space than you need so do not worry if you do not fill all the space.
- Make your final answer clear, and include units if necessary.
- Re-read the questions and check your answers if you have time at the end.

Good luck!

> **Hint**
>
> You can use a pencil and an eraser to make drawings and alter them. But make sure you go over them with a pen when they are finished – your final answers, including drawings, should be in ink.

Combined Science
Paper 1: Biology 1

Time allowed: 1 hour 10 minutes

Answer ALL questions. Write your answers in the spaces provided.

. Catalase is an enzyme found in many different tissues in plants and animals. It speeds up the breakdown of hydrogen peroxide:

hydrogen peroxide → water + oxygen

A group of students wanted to design an experiment to investigate the amount of catalase in different plant and animal tissues. They knew that when the reaction takes place in a test tube, the oxygen gas given off produces foam. They decided that they could measure the height of the foam in the test tube and use this to estimate the amount of catalase in the different types of tissue.

The group was provided with hydrogen peroxide solution, test tubes and five different plant tissues.

(a) Devise a plan, using the supplied solution and apparatus, to compare the amount of enzyme in different tissues.

(3 marks)

....

....

....

....

....

....

Revision Guide pages 7 and 8.

Practical skills Make sure that you say what to add to each test tube – remember that the group are being provided with hydrogen peroxide solution and five different plant tissues. The group have decided that they could measure the height of the foam in the test tube to compare the amount of enzyme in the different types of tissue. You must give the measurements that the students will make when they measure the height of the foam in the test tube.

Exam alert

There are six lines of writing space and three marks available. Use this as a clue as to how much to write.

1

Practical skills To be able to make valid conclusions you must change only one thing – this is your independent variable. Apart from your independent variable, all other variables must be kept the same – these are the control variables.

Hint

Suggest means that you need to apply your knowledge and understanding to a new situation.

Practical skills Accuracy is how close the results are to the true values. The height of the foam is a measurement of enzyme activity. The foam contains the oxygen gas produced in the reaction. Think of a more precise way of measuring the volume of gas produced.

(b) State **two** variables that the students should control in the investigation.

(2 marks)

....

....

....

....

(c) Suggest one improvement that the students could make that would increase the accuracy of their measurement of enzyme activity.

(1 mark)

....

(Total for Question 1 = 6 marks)

. In humans there are two types of cell division: mitosis and meiosis. The table in Figure 1 gives several statements about cell division.

Tick one box in each row to show if the statement is true for mitosis only, for meiosis only or for both mitosis and meiosis. The first row has been completed for you.

(4 marks)

Statement	Mitosis only	Meiosis only	Both mitosis and meiosis
Used for growth and replacement of cells	✓		
Used for production of gametes			
Before the parent cell divides, each chromosome is copied			
Produces genetically identical cells			
Halves the chromosome number			

Figure 1

(Total for Question 2 = 4 marks)

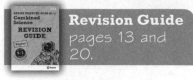

Revision Guide
pages 13 and 20.

Exam alert

This question states 'Tick one box in each row'. You must read the instructions carefully. Use only ticks. If you change your mind, cross out your tick fully, making sure that your new answer is clear.

Explore

Meiosis produces cells that show genetic variation. Mitosis produces cells that are genetically identical to the parent cell. Any variation in cells produced by mitosis is due to mutation. What might cause a mutation?

Hint

You need to say whether the man has a communicable or a non-communicable disease, **and** you need to explain the reasons why. **Explain** means that you need to give a reason for your answer – you need to use your knowledge for this.

LEARN IT!

A communicable disease is infectious – it can pass from person to person. A non-communicable disease is not infectious – it does not pass from person to person.

LEARN IT!

Pathogens cause infectious diseases. Different pathogens cause different diseases.

Hint

You need to be able to name the different types of pathogens – viruses, bacteria, fungi and protists. You should be able to give examples of the symptoms that different pathogens cause.

3. A man has an infection as a result of disease-causing bacteria. He has not been immunised against these bacteria. Figure 2 shows how the number of these bacteria changes after a doctor gives the man a 7-day course of antibiotics.

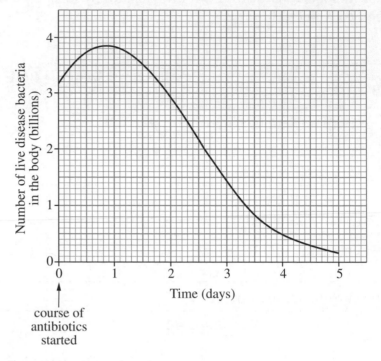

Figure 2

(a) Explain whether the man has a communicable or a non-communicable disease.

(2 marks

....

....

....

....

(b) The man started feeling better on day 3. Calculate the percentage decrease in the number of live, disease-causing microorganisms between the start of the course of antibiotics and the time that the man started to feel better. Give your answer to one decimal place.

(2 marks)

....

(c) The doctor suspected that the disease was caused by a bacterium not a virus. Use the information in the graph to explain why the doctor was correct.

(3 marks)

....

....

....

....

....

....

 Maths skills In **calculate** questions you will be given blank space for working. Use this to write down any calculations that you carry out. You must write down all your working out – even if you get the answer wrong you might still get some marks.

Make sure that you write down at least four decimal places from your calculator before rounding any answers to a suitable degree of accuracy.

 Revision Guide pages 41, 42 and 43

Hint

You must use information from the graph in your answer **and** also use your own knowledge.

Explore

Antibiotics kill only bacteria – they do not kill viruses. There are different types of antibiotics. Why must the correct type of antibiotic be used?

Revision Guide page 46.

Hint

Use the axes titles to help you state the relationship between alcohol consumption and relative risk. When you explain the relationship, you should use numbers from the graph **and** your own knowledge.

This graph shows a **positive correlation** between alcohol consumption and relative risk. This means that, as alcohol consumption increases, the relative risk increases.

(d) Figure 3 shows the results of two studies into the effect of alcohol consumption on the risk of developing liver disease. One group (solid line) consisted only of men and the other group (dotted line) consisted only of women.

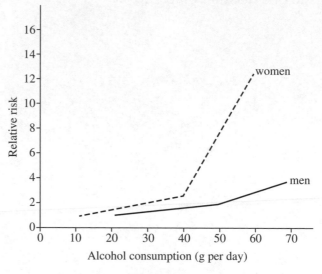

Figure 3

State and explain the relationship between alcohol consumption and relative risk of liver disease for men.

(3 marks)

....

....

....

....

....

....

(Total for Question 3 = 10 marks)

2. (a) Factor VIII is a blood-clotting factor used to treat people with haemophilia. It is now produced in genetically modified bacteria.

Revision Guide
page 34.

    (i)   The factor VIII gene was obtained from human DNA. State the type of enzyme used to cut the factor VIII gene out of the human DNA.

(1 mark)

....

Hint

You do not need to write a full sentence or explain how the enzyme is used – just give the name of the enzyme.

    (ii) The table in Figure 4 shows the processes involved in preparing the genetically modified bacteria, but they are not in the correct order. Complete the table by putting a number in each box to show the correct order. The first one has been completed for you.

(2 marks)

Explore

Restriction enzymes cut the required genes out of DNA. The enzymes leave unpaired bases on the ends of the genes – these are called 'sticky ends'. Why are there different types of restriction enzymes?

Process	Order
A bacterial plasmid is cut open and mixed with the fragments containing the factor VIII gene	
DNA fragments containing the factor VIII gene are prepared	1
DNA ligase joins the sticky ends	
The recombinant plasmid is grown in bacteria to make many copies	
The complementary bases on the sticky ends pair up	

Figure 4

Hint

You can use the space around the box to jot down the order while you are thinking about the answer. Write down the order in the space provided, when you are happy with your answer.

LEARN IT!

You need to know the stages of genetic engineering and the processes used to make genetically modified organisms. You could make a flow chart to learn the stages. Make sure that you know the names and jobs of the enzymes that are used.

Hint

Explain means that you should give the reasons for something happening. The word 'because' is useful in explanations.

Hint

Sticky ends are areas of unpaired bases at the ends of the cut genes. The sticky ends of the required gene and the plasmid are joined by the enzyme DNA ligase.

Revision Guide pages 22 and 23.

Hint

There are many genetic terms that you need to be able to explain. The phenotype of an organism is its characteristics.
The genotype of an organism is the alleles the organism has.

You need to give two letters to represent the alleles for each parent. If the genotypes of each parent are the same, you need to write the genotype only once.

(iii) Explain the importance of sticky ends and DNA ligase in this process.

(3 marks

....

....

....

....

....

....

(b) Cystic fibrosis is an inherited disease caused by a mutated allele for the CFTR protein found in lungs and other tissues. A couple neither of whom had cystic fibrosis, came from families that both had a history of the disease. The couple were concerned that they might have children who were affected. They underwent genetic testing and were found to be heterozygous for the cystic fibrosis gene.

(i) Using F for the normal allele and f for the mutated allele, state the genotype of both parents.

(1 mark

....

Watch out!

You need to use capital and lower case letters clearly. Watch out for this when the letters S and s are used to represent the alleles.

(ii) Predict the percentage probability of the couple's children having cystic fibrosis. Use the Punnett square.

(2 marks)

....

....

(c) Two proteins, DAZL and PRDM14, are involved in the development of sperm cells. Mutations in these genes have been associated with an increased risk of developing testicular cancer. Almost 100% of all testicular cancers can be completely cured if diagnosed early.

Explain how the Human Genome Project has made it possible to improve early diagnosis of diseases, such as testicular cancer, in men with a family history of testicular cancer.

(3 marks)

....

....

....

....

....

....

(Total for Question 4 = 12 marks)

Revision Guide
pages 1 and 2.

5. Figure 5 shows a bacterial cell and a plant cell.

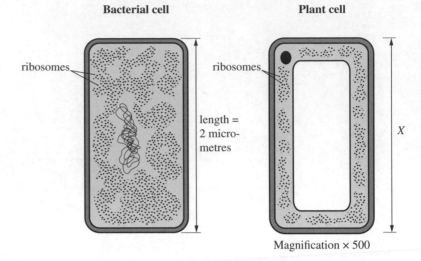

Magnification × 500

Figure 5

(a) (i) Both types of cell contain ribosomes. State the function of a ribosome.

(1 mark

....

(ii) The plant cell contains mitochondria but the bacterial cell does not. State **two** other ways in which the plant cell differs from the bacterial cell.

(2 marks

....

....

Hint

Ribosomes are very small structures that are not visible using a light microscope.

Hint

Make it clear that you are stating how the plant cell differs from the bacterial cell. You could start your answer with 'Plant cells have ...'.

Hint

You need to know the differences between animal cells, plant cells, bacterial cells and yeast cells. You could make a table showing these differences.

(b) Although the cells are drawn the same size, the magnifications are different. The actual length of the bacterial cell is 2 micrometres.

Calculate the actual length, *X*, of the plant cell. Give your answer in micrometres in standard form and to one decimal place. Show your working.

(3 marks)

Revision Guide
pages 3 and 4.

Maths skills To calculate the actual length of the cell you need to rearrange the formula:

$$\text{magnification} = \frac{\text{image size}}{\text{real size}}$$

Hint

Remember to show all your working out – even if you don't get the answer correct, you may still get some marks for your working out.

....

(Total for Question 5 = 6 marks)

Hint

You should read the
sentence at the top
of the chart carefully.
You will need the
information to answer
the question fully.

Hint

Growth is a measure of
a permanent increase
in size – this can be
an increase in mass or
an increase in length.
Growth charts can
be used to monitor
increases in weight and
height of children.

Hint

You need to say what
is being measured
by the doctor or
nurse **and** when the
measurements should
be made. You should
then say how the
doctor or nurse should
use the measurements
with the chart.

6. Figure 6 shows a percentile chart developed by the US government
    to monitor the growth of males between the ages of 2 and 20 years.
    It can be used to monitor both weight and height.

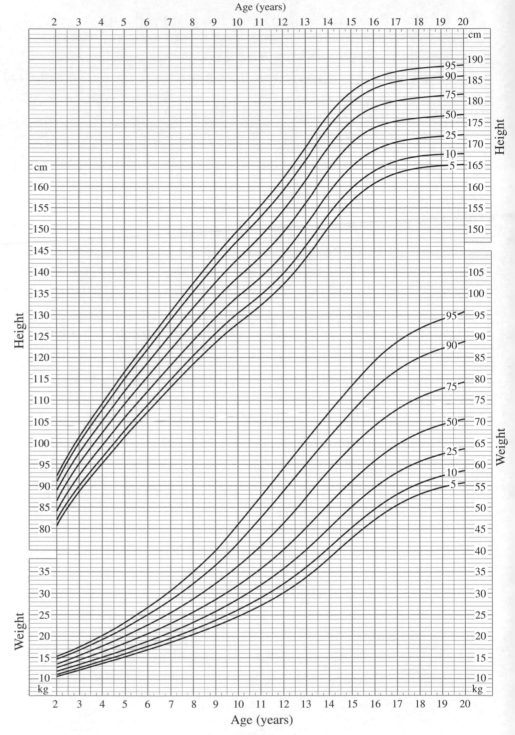

Figure 6

(a) Describe how a doctor or nurse could use this chart to monitor
     the growth of a boy from the age of 2 years to 16 years.

                                                                (3 marks

....

....

(b) The table in Figure 7 shows the weight and height records of two boys, A and B, from the ages of 4 to 16.

Age (years)	Height (cm)		Weight (kg)	
	Boy A	Boy B	Boy A	Boy B
4	102	105	18	17
8	127	132	32	27
12	148	155	56	42
16	170	179	83	60

Figure 7

(i) Plot the height and weight of both boys on the chart on page 12. Use '+' for Boy A and 'o' for Boy B.

(4 marks)

(ii) Use your chart to suggest what conclusions could be made about the development of the two boys.

(4 marks)

....
....
....
....
....
....
....
....

(Total for Question 6 = 11 marks)

Hint

The question has told you to use different symbols for Boy A and Boy B. Make sure that you use the correct symbols. You should not make the symbols too big on the chart.

Hint

You are told only to plot the height and weight of both boys on the chart. You are not told to join the points. Just *do* what the question tells you to.

 Explore

Percentile charts are used to monitor the growth rate of children. Children who are growing too quickly or too slowly can be identified using them. What determines a child's growth rate?

Hint

Suggest means that you need to apply your knowledge to a new situation.

Revision Guide
pages 17 and
18.

LEARN IT!

Reflex reactions are **rapid, involuntary** reactions that protect us from harm or damage.

Hint

You need to remember the order of the neurones in a reflex arc. Remember that the reflex arc starts with a receptor and finishes with an effector. Receptor cells sense stimuli. An effector can be a muscle or a gland.

Hint

Electrical impulses pass along sensory neurones first, then relay neurones, then motor neurones. There are gaps between each type of neurone – called synapses. The electrical impulses cannot pass across the synapses, so chemicals called neurotransmitters diffuse across the synapse, carrying the information from one neurone to the next.

7. Figure 8 shows the neurones and other parts of the body involved in the response to touching a sharp object.

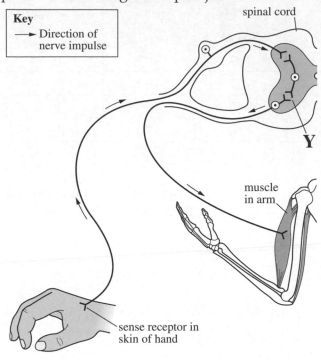

Figure 8

(a) Identify which of the following describes the correct sequence of events after touching a sharp object.

(1 mark)

☐ **A** sensory receptor → sensory neurone → motor neurone → relay neurone

☐ **B** sensory receptor → muscle → motor neurone → relay neurone

☐ **C** sensory receptor → relay neurone → sensory neurone → motor neurone

☐ **D** sensory receptor → sensory neurone → relay neurone → motor neurone

(b) (i) State the name of the structure labelled Y on the diagram.
(1 mark)

....

(ii) Describe the events occurring at point Y that allow the
impulse to be passed on from one neurone to the next.
(3 marks)

....

....

....

....

....

....

Hint

You need to give
only the name for
this question; you do
not need to give any
further information.

Explore

Some drugs affect
the way that synapses
work. Nicotine is a
similar shape to a
neurotransmitter in
the body. Be ready
to explain or suggest
ways in which drugs
may affect the way in
which synapses work.

Revision Guide
page 16.

Hint

Explain means that you need to give reasons for something.
Discuss means you should consider all aspects of the source of stem cells as well as the ethical implications of the different sources.

Explore

There are different types of stem cells: embryonic stem cells, adult stem cells and meristematic stem cells. Where is each type found and of what use is each type?

*(c) Explain how stem cell therapy could be used in the future to treat injuries in the body, such as spinal cord injury. In your answer, you should discuss the sources of stem cells as well as the ethical implications.

(6 marks

....
....
....
....
....
....
....
....
....
....
....
....
....
....
....
....
....
....
....
....

(Total for Question 7 = 11 marks

TOTAL FOR PAPER = 60 MARKS

Combined Science
Paper 2: Biology

Time allowed: 1 hour 10 minutes

Answer ALL questions. Write your answers in the spaces provided.

1. (a) A student carried out an investigation into osmosis in potato pieces. The student cut five pieces of potato, weighed them and then placed them into different concentrations of salt solution. After one hour the student removed the potato pieces from the salt solution and weighed them again. The student's results are shown in the table in Figure 1.

Concentration of salt solution (mol dm⁻³)	Initial mass of potato (g)	Final mass of potato (g)	Percentage change in mass (%)
0.0	5.2	5.4	
0.25	5.6	5.6	
0.5	5.6	5.4	
1.0	5.0	4.6	
1.5	5.2	4.2	

Figure 1

(i) Complete the table by calculating the percentage change in mass of the potato pieces. Give your answers to 1 decimal place.

(3 marks)

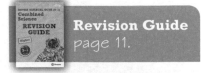

Revision Guide page 11.

 Practical skills The independent variable is the concentration of salt solution – this is what the student is choosing to change in the experiment. The dependent variable is the change in mass of the potato pieces. If you do this experiment you should gently blot the potato pieces with a paper towel to remove any excess solution.

Maths skills To calculate the percentage change in mass you need to use the equation:

$$\text{percentage change} = \frac{\text{change in mass}}{\text{initial mass}} \times 100$$

Maths skills Remember to show all your working out – if you get the answer wrong you could still get some marks.

(ii) Give one step the student should take to increase the accuracy and repeatability of the measurements.

(1 mark

....

....

(iii) Use your results from part (i) to estimate the solute concentration of the potato cells.

(1 mark

....

(b) Figure 2 shows the part of the lung where gas exchange takes place.

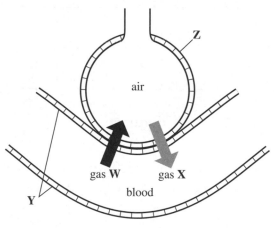

Figure 2

(i) State the names of the structures labelled **Y** and **Z** in the diagram.

(2 marks)

Structure Y is the ....

Structure Z is the ....

(ii) Which one of the following methods describes how gases W and X move in the directions shown?

(1 mark)

☐ **A** diffusion

☐ **B** osmosis

☐ **C** breathing

☐ **D** respiration

(iii) State the name of gas X.

(1 mark)

....

(c) A scientist recently estimated that the average human lung has 480 million alveoli and that 1 million alveoli have a surface area of 0.15 m².

Calculate the total surface area of a human lung.

(2 marks)

(Total for Question 1 = 11 marks)

Watch out!

This question is asking you to calculate the total surface area of a human lung – that is **one** human lung.

 **Maths skills** Remember to show all of your working out – if you get the answer wrong you could still get some marks.

🔍 **Explore**

Multicellular organisms are large and require special organs to exchange substances with their environment. Think about how exchange surfaces in these organs are adapted for their roles.

Revision Guide
page 74.

Hint

You need to give an approximate value for this person's resting heart rate. You should identify when the man is resting and read off the heart rate.

Hint

When the man is exercising, the heart rate will increase. You need to find the time when the man started to exercise.

Hint

You need to give numbers from the graph as evidence.

Hint

Explain means that you have to give reasons for something happening. The word 'because' is useful in explain questions.

2. Figure 3 shows the heart rate of an adult male over a 24-hour period.

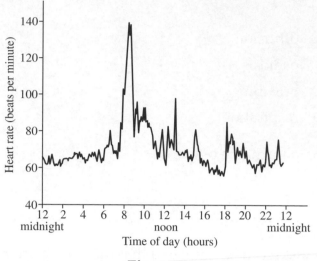

Figure 3

(a) (i) Use the graph to estimate this person's resting heart rate.

(1 mark)

....

(ii) The man attended a one hour spinning (indoor cycling) class during the day. Use the graph to estimate the start time of the class.

(1 mark)

....

(iii) About an hour before the class started the man walked uphill to the gym where the class was held. He then rested until the class started.

Give one piece of evidence from the trace that supports this.

(1 mark)

....

....

(iv) The man noticed that his heart rate remained higher than normal for some time after the end of the class.

Explain why his heart rate remained high.

(2 marks)

....

....

....

(b) (i) The table in Figure 4 shows the stroke volume and heart rate for two people measured while they were at rest.

Complete the table by calculating the cardiac output for each person. Include the units for cardiac output.

(3 marks)

	Stroke volume (cm³)	Heart rate (beats/min)	Cardiac output	Units
Person A	95	52		
Person B	58	72		

Figure 4

(ii) One of these people was a trained athlete, the other was untrained. Suggest and explain which is the trained athlete.

(2 marks)

....

....

....

....

(Total for Question 2 = 10 marks)

Watch out!

You have been given units for stroke volume and heart rate – use these to give the units for cardiac output.

Maths skills Remember to show all of your working out – if you do not get the answer correct you could still get some marks.

Maths skills You need to use the equation:
cardiac output = stroke volume × heart rate

Hint

Suggest means that you need to apply your knowledge to a new situation.

Hint

Your cells are respiring all the time. When you exercise, **more** respiration occurs so cells need **more** oxygen and glucose and produce **more** carbon dioxide, water and energy.

 **Explore**

What are the effects of exercise on the body? You need to be able to use terms such as cardiac output, heart rate and stroke volume to describe these effects.

Revision Guide
pages 58–62.

Hint

State means that you just need to name the place where it is produced.

Hint

Describe means that you need to give some facts about what FSH does to the ovary.

Watch out!

You need to know that clomifene is a drug that is used in assisted reproductive therapy.

Hint

You need to give reasons why clomifene helps women to increase their fertility.

LEARN IT!

Fertility is the ability to become pregnant.

LEARN IT!

Ovulation is the release of mature egg cells from the ovaries.

3. (a) The term assisted reproductive therapy (ART) covers a number of treatments to help couples who are having difficulty conceiving a child. Various hormones and drugs are used in ART. One such hormone is FSH.

   (i) State where FSH is produced.

   (1 mark)

   ....

   (ii) Describe the effect of FSH on the ovary.

   (1 mark)

   ....

   (b) The drug clomifene can be used to treat women who have difficulty conceiving.

   (i) Explain how clomifene can help such women conceive.

   (2 marks)

   ....

   ....

   ....

   ....

   (ii) Explain why clomifene is used to stimulate ovulation in women undergoing IVF, even if they ovulate naturally.

   (2 marks)

   ....

   ....

   ....

   ....

   (Total for Question 3 = 6 marks)

Adrenalin and noradrenalin are chemically similar molecules. However, adrenalin is a hormone and noradrenalin is a neurotransmitter.

(a) State the organ where adrenalin is produced.

(1 mark)

....

(b) Describe how adrenalin reaches its target organs.

(2 marks)

....

....

....

....

(c) Describe **two** ways in which hormonal communication is different to nervous communication.

(2 marks)

....

....

....

....

Revision Guide pages 17, 18, 58 and 59.

LEARN IT!

Neurotransmitters carry the nerve impulse across the synapse (gap between neurones) because electrical impulses cannot pass across synapses. They cause an electrical impulse in the next neurone.

Watch out!

Hormones travel in the blood. Neurotransmitters travel in the fluid between neurones.

Hint

Describe means that you need to give facts about each type of communication. The facts need to show how the types of communication are different.

Watch out!

This question says 'state the name of one **other** hormone that has the same effect'. You must be careful not to use adrenalin as the hormone, because the question has already used that example.

 **Explore**

There are two different types of diabetes – Type 1 and Type 2. Type 1 diabetes occurs when the pancreas has been damaged and does not produce insulin or not enough insulin. Type 2 diabetes occurs when a person produces insulin but the target cells have become resistant to it. Why do these types of diabetes happen and how are they treated?

(d) Adrenalin causes muscle cells to convert glycogen to glucose.

    (i)   State the name of one other hormone that has the same effect.

(1 mark)

....

    (ii)   State the name of the disease caused by the body not being able to regulate the concentration of glucose in the blood.

(1 mark)

....

(Total for Question 4 = 7 marks)

5. An epiphyte is a plant that grows harmlessly on another plant, and obtains its water and nutrients from the air, rain and debris that accumulate around it.

Revision Guide
page 78.

(a) Mistletoe is a parasitic plant. Explain how a parasite differs from an epiphyte.

(3 marks)

....

....

....

....

....

....

Hint

A parasite feeds on another organism, which is called the host.

(b) Nitrogen-fixing bacteria grow in the root nodules of legumes. Explain why nitrogen-fixing bacteria are considered to be mutualists rather than parasites.

(3 marks)

....

....

....

....

....

....

(Total for Question 5 = 6 marks)

Watch out!

In parasitic relationships, only one of the organisms benefits; the other is harmed. In mutualistic relationships, both organisms benefit.

Explore

Give some examples of parasitic and mutualistic relationships.

Revision Guide
pages 76 and
77.

Watch out!

Abiotic factors are
'non-living' factors.
Biotic factors are
'living' factors.

6. A group of students were undertaking a survey of an area of land alongside a path that crossed a field and entered a piece of woodland.

   (a) (i) State **two** abiotic factors that might influence the distribution of plant species in the woodland.

   (2 marks

   ....

   ....

   (ii) State **two** biotic factors that might influence the distribution of plant species next to the path in the field.

   (2 marks

   ....

   ....

*(b) Describe how the students should survey the abundance of different plant species growing alongside the path from the field and into the wood.

(6 marks)

....

....

....

....

....

....

....

....

....

....

....

....

....

....

(Total for Question 6 = 10 marks)

Hint

Describe means that you need to give facts about how the students should survey the different plant species. You need to use your knowledge of fieldwork techniques to do this. You must include how to record and display the results.

Watch out!

The students need to survey the abundance of different plant species – abundance means the number of each different plant species.

Explore

When would you randomly sample an area or sample along a transect?

Which biotic and abiotic factors would you measure?

How could you record and display results?

Revision Guide
pages 1, 2 and
53.

Watch out!

Read the information at the start of the question carefully – this question tells you that the diagram shows a specialised type of **plant** tissue.

Hint

You just need to place a cross in the box next to the correct letter for your answer.

Hint

Identify means that you need to name the parts labelled E and F.

Hint

You need to say what the function of mitochondria is, what is produced by the mitochondria and what the companion cells use this for.

7. (a) Figure 5 shows a specialised type of plant tissue.

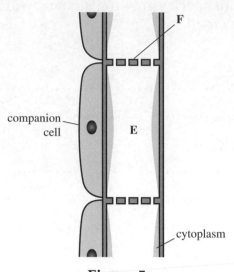

Figure 5

(i) Which specialised plant tissue is shown in Figure 5?

(1 mark

☐ **A** xylem

☐ **B** phloem

☐ **C** mesophyll

☐ **D** root hair

(ii) Identify the parts labelled E and F.

(2 marks

E is a ....

F is a ....

(iii) Explain why the companion cell contains large numbers of mitochondria.

(3 marks

....

....

....

....

....

....

Revision Guide
pages 50, 51
and 52

(b) (i) Temperature can be a limiting factor in photosynthesis.
State **one** other factor that can limit the rate of
photosynthesis.

(1 mark)

....

(ii) Figure 6 shows how the rate of photosynthesis changes
as temperature is increased. Explain how the rate of
photosynthesis changes as the temperature is increased.

(3 marks)

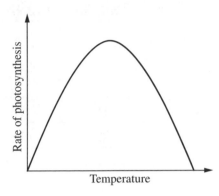

Figure 6

....
....
....
....
....
....

(Total for Question 7 = 10 marks)

TOTAL FOR PAPER = 60 MARKS

Watch out!

There are a number
of different answers
here; you just need
to give one factor,
but you cannot give
temperature – they
have already given this
factor in the question.

Hint

It does not matter
which of these answers
you choose to give.

Hint

Explain means that
you have to give
reasons why the rate
of photosynthesis
changes as the
temperature is
increased. You need
to explain what
happens when the rate
of photosynthesis
increases, then
decreases, as the
temperature increases.

Explore

Photosynthesis is an
enzyme-controlled
reaction. Use your
knowledge of how
enzymes work to
explain how the rate
of photosynthesis
changes with a change
in temperature.

Combined Science
Paper 3: Chemistry 1

Time allowed: 1 hour 10 minutes

Answer ALL questions. Write your answers in the spaces provided.

1. (a) The table in Figure 1 gives the numbers of protons, neutrons and electrons in five different particles (**V, W, X, Y** and **Z**).

Particle	Protons	Neutrons	Electrons
V	8	8	8
W	11	12	11
X	13	14	10
Y	15	16	18
Z	18	22	18

Figure 1

(i) Which particle is a positively charged **ion**?

(1 mark)

☐ **A** particle W

☐ **B** particle X

☐ **C** particle Y

☐ **D** particle Z

(ii) Which particles are **atoms** of non-metals?

(1 mark)

☐ **A** particles V and W

☐ **B** particles W and X

☐ **C** particles X and Y

☐ **D** particles V and Z

Revision Guide
pages 92 and 96.

Hint

All five particles contain different numbers of protons, so none of them can be isotopes of one element.

Hint

Ions form when atoms (or groups of atoms) lose or gain electrons.

Hint

It will help if you look at a periodic table to identify metals and non-metals.

Exam alert

Make sure that you answer multiple-choice questions, even if you are not certain that you are correct.

(b) A sample of neon consists of 90.5% $_{10}^{20}$Ne and 9.5% $_{10}^{22}$Ne.

(i) Describe, in terms of subatomic particles, why these are isotopes of the same element.

(4 marks)

....

....

....

....

(ii) Calculate the relative atomic mass, A_r, of this sample of neon. Give your answer to one decimal place.

(3 marks)

Relative atomic mass =.............

(Total for Question 1 = 9 marks)

Revision Guide
page 95.

LEARN IT!

Atomic number is the number of protons in a nucleus, which is equal to the number of electrons in an atom.

Hint

Use the periodic table to find the atomic number of phosphorus. This will give you the number of electrons in its atoms.

Hint

What do the electronic configurations have in common, and how is this linked to the group number?

Hint

How do their electronic configurations differ, and how is this linked to the period numbers?

Explore

The electronic configuration of an element is related to its position in the modern periodic table. This was unknown in Mendeleev's time, so Mendeleev organised his table differently.

2. This question is about electrons and the periodic table.

(a) Complete the diagram below to show the electronic configuration of phosphorus, P.

(1 mark

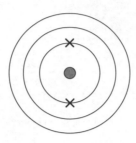

(b) State, in terms of their electronic configurations, why fluorine and chlorine are placed in group 7.

(1 mark

....

....

(c) Explain, in terms of their electronic configurations, why magnesium is in period 3 but calcium is in period 4.

(2 marks

....

....

....

....

(Total for Question 2 = 4 marks

3. The table in Figure 2 gives the formulae of three ions.

Name of ion	Formula of ion
aluminium	Al^{3+}
hydroxide	OH^-
sulfate	SO_4^{2-}

Figure 2

Revision Guide
pages 89, 96,
97 and 109.

(a) Which of these is the correct formula for aluminium sulfate?

(1 mark)

☐ **A** Al_3SO_4

☐ **B** $Al_3(SO_4)_2$

☐ **C** $Al_2(SO_4)_3$

☐ **D** Al_2SO_4

LEARN IT!

The numbers of each ion in the formula for an ionic compound must give equal numbers of positive and negative charges.

(b) The atomic number of fluorine is 9 and its mass number is 19. Calculate the numbers of protons, neutrons and electrons in a fluoride ion, F^-.

(3 marks)

Protons...

Neutrons...

Electrons...

Maths skills The numbers of protons, neutrons and electrons in atoms and ions are always integers (whole numbers).

(c) Aluminium sulfate is soluble in water. It is used in the treatmen
of water for drinking.

Maths skills The volume
is given in cm³ but the
concentration is in
g dm⁻³. Remember to
convert from cm³ to
dm³ in your calculation.

(i)   A solution of aluminium sulfate is formed by dissolving
35 g of aluminium sulfate in 250 cm³ of water.

Calculate the concentration, in g dm⁻³, of this solution.

(2 marks

Hint

Write the formulae of
the two reacting ions,
and the formula for
aluminium hydroxide.
Then add a balancing
number where needed.

For the state symbols,
look at the information
given to work out which
are in aqueous solution
and which are solid.

(ii)   A precipitate of aluminium hydroxide is produced during
the treatment of water. This sticky solid traps other small
pieces of insoluble solid, so they sink to the bottom of the
water treatment tank.

Write a balanced ionic equation for the reaction between
aluminium ions and hydroxide ions in solution to form
aluminium hydroxide. Include state symbols.

(3 marks

(Total for Question 3 = 9 marks

Air is a mixture of gases, including nitrogen, oxygen and carbon dioxide.

(a) Why does nitrogen have a low boiling point?

(1 mark)

☐ **A** There are weak forces of attraction between nitrogen molecules.

☐ **B** There are weak covalent bonds between nitrogen molecules.

☐ **C** There are weak forces of attraction between nitrogen atoms.

☐ **D** There are weak covalent bonds between nitrogen atoms.

(b) Explain how a covalent bond forms.

(2 marks)

....

....

....

....

(c) Draw a dot-and-cross diagram to show a molecule of carbon dioxide, CO_2. Show the outer electrons only.

(2 marks)

Revision Guide
pages 99–101.

🔍 **Explore**

Ionic compounds, giant covalent substances and metals have high melting points and boiling points. This is due to the different strong bonds that are broken or overcome during melting and boiling.

Hint

Covalent bonding does not involve the formation of ions.

Hint

Draw a circle for each atom, overlapping them where you want to show the bonding electrons. Show a solid dot for each electron from one element and a cross for each electron from the other element.

Watch out!

Make sure that you also include dots or crosses for any electrons **not** involved in bonding.

(d) Figure 3 shows the structures of diamond and graphite.

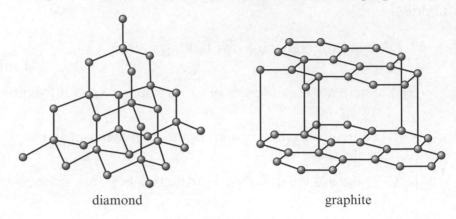

diamond   graphite

Figure 3

Explain, in terms of structure and bonding, why diamond has a very high melting point.

(2 marks)

....

....

....

....

(Total for Question 4 = 7 marks)

A student adds magnesium to an excess of dilute hydrochloric acid in an evaporating basin. Magnesium chloride solution and hydrogen gas form. When the reaction is complete, the student carefully evaporates the magnesium chloride solution to dryness. The table in Figure 4 shows her results.

Revision Guide
page 106.

Object	Mass (g)
empty evaporating basin	86.43
evaporating basin with magnesium	87.64
magnesium used	
evaporating basin with magnesium chloride	91.22
magnesium chloride formed	

Figure 4

(a) Complete the table to show the mass of magnesium used, and the mass of magnesium chloride formed.

(2 marks)

Hint

You are given the mass of the empty basin, and its mass when it contains magnesium or magnesium chloride.

(b) Use your answers to part (a) to calculate the mass of chlorine present in the magnesium chloride.

(1 mark)

Hint

Magnesium and chlorine are the only elements present in magnesium chloride.

Mass of chlorine = ... g

LEARN IT!

An empirical formula
is the simplest whole
number ratio of atoms
of each element in a
substance.

Hint

For each element,
divide its mass by its
A,. Then divide both
values obtained by the
smallest value to help
you find the smallest
whole number ratio.

Watch out!

Remember to write
down the empirical
formula after doing the
calculations.

(c) Use your answers to parts (a) and (b) to calculate the **empirical formula** of magnesium chloride.
(Relative atomic masses: Mg = 24, Cl = 35.5)

(3 marks)

Empirical formula = ...

(Total for Question 5 = 6 marks

This question is about drinking water.

(a) Which of these describes clean drinking water?

(1 mark)

- ☐ **A** a pure substance
- ☐ **B** a simple molecular compound
- ☐ **C** a mixture of substances
- ☐ **D** not potable

(b) Drinking water can be made by the simple distillation of seawater.

(i) Describe, in terms of the arrangement and relative energy of water particles, what happens when water boils.

(2 marks)

....

....

....

(ii) Explain why distilled water, rather than tap water, is suitable for use in chemical analysis.

(2 marks)

....

....

....

(c) Fresh water can be made safe for drinking at a water treatment plant. Sedimentation is needed to allow small particles to settle out. Filtration and chlorination are also needed.

(i) Describe why filtration is needed.

(1 mark)

....

....

(ii) Explain why chlorination is needed.

(2 marks)

....

....

(Total for Question 6 = 8 marks)

Revision Guide
pages 121–126.

LEARN IT!

All common nitrates are soluble, and so are common sodium, potassium and ammonium salts.

Hint

A precipitate is an insoluble substance formed in a reaction.

LEARN IT!

The pH increases by 1 when the H^+ ion concentration decreases by a factor of 10.

Watch out!

The words 'strong' and 'weak' do not imply that the acids are 'concentrated' and 'dilute'. Make sure that you are clear about the differences.

---

7. This question is about making salts.

(a) Which row in the table correctly identifies a soluble substance and an insoluble substance?

(1 mark)

	Soluble in water	Insoluble in water
☐ A	silver chloride	lead chloride
☐ B	sodium carbonate	calcium sulfate
☐ C	sodium chloride	calcium chloride
☐ D	barium sulfate	barium nitrate

(b) Predict whether a precipitate will form when sodium hydroxide solution and iron(III) chloride solution are mixed together. Name any precipitate that forms.

(1 mark)

....

(c) Aqueous solutions can be acidic, neutral or alkaline.

(i) State the type of aqueous solution that contains an excess of hydroxide ions, $OH^-(aq)$.

(1 mark)

....

(ii) An acidic solution, with a pH of 0.70, contains 0.20 mol dm^{-3} of hydrogen ions, $H^+(aq)$.

Predict the pH of an acidic solution that contains 0.020 mol dm^{-3} of $H^+(aq)$.

(1 mark)

....

(iii) Explain, in terms of ions, the difference between a strong acid and a weak acid.

(2 marks)

....

....

....

*(d) Plan an experiment to prepare pure, dry, hydrated crystals of copper chloride, $CuCl_2$, from an insoluble copper compound and a suitable dilute acid. In your answer, include the names of suitable reagents and describe any essential stages. You may wish to write a balanced equation to help with your plan.

(6 marks)

....
....
....
....
....
....
....
....
....
....
....
....
....
....

(Total for Question 7 = 12 marks)

Practical skills One of the Core Practicals is the preparation of pure, dry, hydrated copper sulfate crystals, starting from copper oxide. This is a similar practical. Make sure that you include the main steps in your answer.

Hint

Many metal oxides and metal carbonates are insoluble in water.

Explore

Soluble substances are used to make insoluble salts by precipitation and some soluble salts are made using titration.

Revision Guide
pages 128–131.

Hint

Learn definitions of objects and processes. These usually start with 'Recall' in the specification.

Hint

It may help to work out first if copper or chlorine forms at the negative electrode.

LEARN IT!

Electrolysis is a process in which electrical energy, from a direct current supply, decomposes electrolytes.

Hint

You need to add a number to each space. Do not change any of the formulae that you are given.

Explore

Most metals are extracted from compounds found in ores. The method used depends on the metal's position in the reactivity series and the cost of the process itself.

---

8. This question is about electrolysis.

(a) State what is meant by the term **electrolyte**.

(2 marks)

....

....

(b) Copper and chlorine form during the electrolysis of concentrated copper chloride solution. Which row in the table correctly shows what happens at the negative electrode?

(1 mark)

	Product formed	Type of reaction
☐ A	copper	reduction
☐ B	copper	oxidation
☐ C	chlorine	reduction
☐ D	chlorine	oxidation

(c) Aluminium is extracted by the electrolysis of aluminium oxide, dissolved in molten cryolite.

(i) State why aluminium cannot be extracted from aluminium oxide by heating with carbon.

(1 mark)

....

....

(ii) Balance the half equation below for the reaction that occurs at the anode.

(1 mark)

..... $O^{2-} \rightarrow O_2 +$ ..... e^-

(Total for Question 8 = 5 marks)

TOTAL FOR PAPER = 60 MARKS

Combined Science
Paper 4: Chemistry 2

Time: 1 hour 10 minutes

Answer ALL questions. Write your answers in the spaces provided.

1. This question is about the alkali metals, the elements in group 1 of the periodic table.

   (a) Which of these shows the typical physical properties of the alkali metals?

   (1 mark)

   ☐ **A** soft with relatively low melting points

   ☐ **B** soft with relatively high melting points

   ☐ **C** hard with relatively low melting points

   ☐ **D** hard with relatively high melting points

   (b) Potassium reacts with water. The reaction produces potassium hydroxide solution, KOH, and hydrogen gas, H_2.

   (i) Write the balanced equation for the reaction between potassium and water.

   (2 marks)

   (ii) Describe what is seen when a piece of potassium is added to a trough of water.

   (2 marks)

   ....

   ....

Revision Guide
page 143.

Hint

It may help to consider whether the alkali metals are soft or hard metals.

Watch out!

Make sure that you answer multiple-choice questions, even if you are not certain that you are correct.

Hint

You are given the formula needed except the formulae for potassium and water. You are not asked for state symbols.

Watch out!

Make sure that you write about what you would **see** during the reaction, not why the substances react together or the names of any products formed.

You should be able to predict the electronic configurations of the first 20 elements in the periodic table both as diagrams and as numbers.

Hint

What happens to their reactivity as you go down the group? Think about what happens to metal atoms when metals react, and how that is related to their sizes and their outer electrons.

(c) The electronic configuration of lithium is 2.1.

(i) Write the electronic configurations of sodium and potassium.

(2 marks)

sodium......................................

potassium................................

(ii) Explain the trend in the reactivity of the group 1 metals.

(3 marks)

....
....
....
....
....
....

(Total for Question 1 = 10 marks)

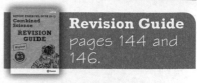
2. This question is about the halogens, the elements in group 7 of the periodic table.

(a) Which row in the table correctly shows the colours and physical states of the halogens at room temperature and pressure?

(1 mark)

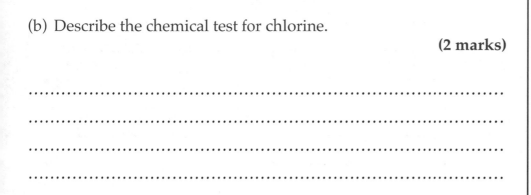

	Chlorine	Bromine	Iodine
A	pale yellow liquid	red–brown liquid	red–brown solid
B	yellow–green gas	purple liquid	purple-black solid
C	yellow–green gas	red–brown liquid	purple-black solid
D	yellow–green gas	purple liquid	red–brown liquid

(b) Describe the chemical test for chlorine.

(2 marks)

....

....

....

....

Revision Guide
pages 144 and 146.

LEARN IT!

The melting points and boiling points of the halogens increase going down group 7.

Practical skills Write down the names of the substances you would need to carry out the test, and what you expect to observe.

Explore

Displacement reactions
such as this one can
be used to determine
a reactivity series for
the halogens.

Hint

A more reactive
halogen can oxidise the
halide ions of a less
reactive halogen.

Watch out!

In terms of oxygen,
oxidation is a gain of
oxygen and reduction
is a loss of oxygen.
This question is instead
about oxidation and
reduction in terms of
electrons.

*(c) In aqueous solution, chlorine reacts with sodium iodide, NaI.
Sodium chloride solution and iodine solution form:

$$Cl_2 + 2NaI \rightarrow 2NaCl + I_2$$

Explain, in terms of electron gain and loss, why this reaction is a
redox reaction. You may include half equations in your answer.

(6 marks)

....

....

....

....

....

....

....

....

....

....

(Total for Question 2 = 9 marks)

3. A student investigates the rate of reaction between calcium carbonate (marble chips) and excess dilute hydrochloric acid:

$$CaCO_3(s) + 2HCl(aq) \rightarrow CaCl_2(aq) + H_2O(l) + CO_2(g)$$

(a) Which of these would increase the rate of reaction?

(1 mark)

- ☐ **A** adding water to the acid
- ☐ **B** increasing the volume of acid
- ☐ **C** increasing the size of the marble chips
- ☐ **D** using calcium carbonate powder instead of marble chips

(b) The student added 0.50 g of calcium carbonate to 50 cm³ of 0.40 mol dm⁻³ hydrochloric acid. Show, by calculation, that the acid is in excess. (Relative formula mass of $CaCO_3$ = 100)

(4 marks)

Amount of HCl =............... mol

Revision Guide pages 149 and 150.

🧪 **Practical skills** Remember that you should also be able to suggest practical methods to determine the rate of a given reaction.

🔢 **Maths skills** You can calculate the amount of $CaCO_3$ from the mass and relative formula mass.

🔢 **Maths skills** You can calculate the amount of HCl from the concentration and volume (in dm³) of the acid.

Hint

Once you know the amounts of both substances, look back at the balanced equation to see the ratio that reacts.

(c) The student measured the volume of carbon dioxide produced until all the calcium carbonate had reacted. Figure 1 shows the results that she obtained at 20 °C.

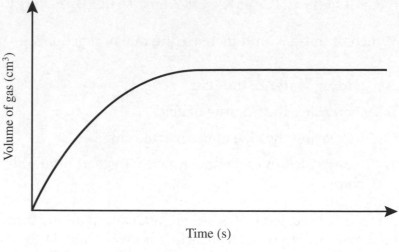

Figure 1

Watch out!

There are two marks for this question, so the shape of your line must have at least two required features.

(i) Sketch, on the same axes above, the results that the student would obtain by repeating the experiment at a higher temperature.

(2 marks

(ii) Explain, in terms of particles, why increasing the temperature has this effect on the rate of reaction.

(3 marks

....

....

....

....

....

....

(Total for Question 3 = 10 marks

Hint

Reactions happen when particles collide. Think about what happens to the frequency and energy of collisions when reacting substances are heated.

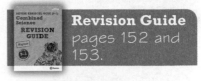

Revision Guide
pages 152 and
153.

. Hydrogen peroxide solution decomposes to form water and oxygen:

$$2H_2O_2(aq) \rightarrow 2H_2O(l) + O_2(g)$$

The reaction is exothermic.

(a) Draw and label the reaction profile diagram for this reaction on Figure 2. Label the activation energy.

(3 marks)

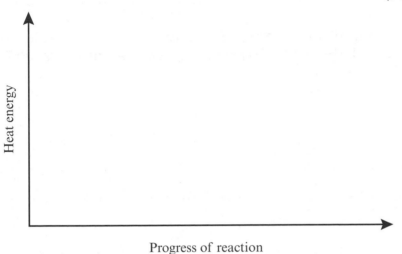

Progress of reaction

Figure 2

(b) Manganese dioxide, MnO_2, acts as a catalyst for this reaction.

(i) On the same axes as above, draw the reaction profile for the same reaction in the presence of a catalyst. Label this line with an **X**.

(1 mark)

🔍 **Explore**

Exothermic and endothermic reactions have different features, including the overall direction of energy transfer and changes in temperature.

Watch out!

Make sure that you label the reactants and products, and clearly label the part of your diagram that represents activation energy.

Watch out!

Remember to label this second line clearly as **X**.

Hint

Remember that catalysts speed up reactions but are unchanged chemically and in mass at the end of the reaction. How do they do this?

Hint

What does the rapid bubbling show? What could liver contain that causes this to happen?

(ii) Explain, in terms of energy, how a catalyst works.

(2 marks

....

....

....

....

(c) If a piece of raw liver is added to hydrogen peroxide solution, rapid bubbling is observed. Suggest reasons that explain this observation.

(2 marks

....

....

....

....

(Total for Question 4 = 8 marks

5. Ethene undergoes complete combustion in oxygen to form carbon dioxide and water as shown in Figure 3:

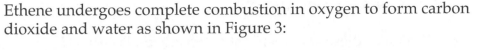

Figure 3

Revision Guide page 154.

(a) The energies of some bonds are shown in Figure 4. Calculate the energy change for the complete combustion of 1 mol of ethene.

(4 marks)

Bond	Bond energy (kJ mol^{-1})
C–H	413
O=O	498
C=O	805
C=C	612
O–H	464

Figure 4

Energy change = ………… kJ mol^{-1}

(b) Explain, in terms of the energy involved in breaking bonds and making bonds, why this reaction is exothermic.

(2 marks)

....

....

....

....

(Total for Question 5 = 6 marks)

Revision Guide pages 155 and 156.

Hint

A non-renewable resource is one that is being used up faster than it can be replaced.

LEARN IT!

You should be able to recall the names and uses of the fractions shown in the diagram.

 **Explore**

The substances in different fractions belong to the same homologous series, but differ in the number of atoms in their molecules. They also differ in their boiling points, ease of ignition and viscosity.

Watch out!

Identify means that you must give an answer using the information given. In these questions, this is the names of crude oil fractions and where they leave the fractionating column. The position in which an individual fraction leaves the column gives a clue as to its physical properties, in this case its boiling point.

6. This question is about crude oil.

(a) Which of these statements about crude oil is correct?

(1 mark)

☐ **A** It is a renewable resource.

☐ **B** It contains molecules with carbon atoms in rings and chains.

☐ **C** It is a complex mixture of carbohydrates.

☐ **D** At room temperature, it contains only liquids.

(b) Crude oil is separated into fractions using fractional distillation. Figure 5 shows an oil-fractionating column and the main fractions obtained from it.

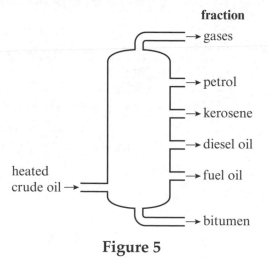

Figure 5

Identify the fraction which:

(i) has the highest boiling point

(1 mark)

....

(ii) is used as a fuel for aircraft.

(1 mark)

....

(c) State why crude oil may be described as a finite resource.

(1 mark)

....

....

(d) Explain how the different substances in crude oil are separated by fractional distillation.

(4 marks)

....

....

....

....

....

....

....

....

(Total for Question 6 = 8 marks)

Hint

This is not the same as a non-renewable resource, although these resources are usually also finite.

Watch out!

Describe means that you need to give an account of something without giving reasons. However, this is an **Explain** question, so you also need to say **why** things happen.

Revision Guide
pages 163 and
164.

Watch out!

Read questions
carefully. This one is
not about today's
atmosphere.

Hint

Write down whether
the amount has
increased, decreased
or stayed the same.
Then give two ways in
which this happened.

Practical skills Write
down what you would
do, including the
names of necessary
substances, and what
you expect to observe.

Explore

There is evidence that
human activities are
leading to increased
levels of carbon
dioxide and methane,
and that this is a cause
of climate change.
You should be able
to evaluate evidence
for this, its potential
effects, and how these
could be reduced or
overcome.

7. This question is about the Earth's atmosphere.

    (a) Which of these gases was the most abundant in the Earth's
        earliest atmosphere?

        (1 mark

        ☐ **A**   nitrogen
        ☐ **B**   oxygen
        ☐ **C**   argon
        ☐ **D**   carbon dioxide

    (b) Explain how the amount of carbon dioxide in the atmosphere
        changed over geological time.

        (3 marks

        ....

        ....

        ....

        ....

        ....

    (c) The combustion of fossil fuels needs oxygen, found in air.

        (i)   Describe the chemical test for oxygen.

              (2 marks

              ....

              ....

              ....

              ....

        (ii) The combustion of fossil fuels releases carbon dioxide into
              the air. Explain how this gas could cause a change in the
              temperature of the Earth.

              (3 marks

              ....

              ....

              ....

              ....

              ....

        (Total for Question 7 = 9 marks)

        TOTAL FOR PAPER = 60 MARKS

Combined Science
Practice Paper 5: Physics 1

Time allowed: 1 hour 10 minutes

Answer ALL questions. Write your answers in the spaces provided.

1. Robert and Nolly plan to set up an experiment to measure speed.
   They have a trolley, an inclined ramp, a ruler and a stopwatch.

   (a) Describe a method that the students could use to measure the
   speed of the trolley using the apparatus above.

   (3 marks)

   ....

   ....

   ....

   ....

   ....

   ....

   (b) Suggest other apparatus that the students could use to improve
   the precision of the data collected.

   (2 marks)

   ....

   ....

Revision Guide
pages 168–171.

Hint

Read the list of apparatus carefully. Use all the apparatus, and nothing else.

Practical skills Sketch and label a diagram and then say how the apparatus will be used.

Hint

Don't ramble! Give clear, concise points.

Exam alert

There are two marks here, so you need two pieces of apparatus.

Practical skills Think about the biggest cause of uncertainty in the experiment then suggest what could be used to get round that problem.

Hint

The independent variable
is the one the person
doing the experiment
chooses the values of.
Look for one that goes
up in regular steps.

Hint

Look back at the aim of
the experiment at the
start of the question
to work out what you
might need to help with
the analysis.

**Maths
skills** You will have
to calculate the correct
entries. Choose the
appropriate formula,
write in the values
and then work out the
answer.

(c) Robert and Nolly then extend their experiment to investigate
the influence of another independent variable. The table in
Figure 1 shows data collected by the students.

(cm)	(m)	(s)	
5	1.80	3.2	0.56
10	1.80	2.4	
15	1.80	1.8	1.0
20	1.80	1.4	1.29
25	1.80	1.0	
30	1.80	0.4	4.5
35	1.80	0.2	9.0

Figure 1

(i) Deduce what the new independent variable might be and
add titles for all **three** completed columns in the table.

(1 mark

....

(ii) Add a fourth column heading, with units, that could be
added to the table to help with analysis. Add the **two**
missing entries for the fourth column.

(1 mark

*(d) After travelling down the ramp, the trolley comes to a stop by itself. Discuss factors that would have caused the trolley to come to a stop and how these factors could be reduced.

(6 marks)

....

....

....

....

....

....

....

....

....

....

....

....

....

(Total for Question 1 = 13 marks)

Hint

Make sure that you structure your answer clearly. State a factor and then say how it could be reduced. Then, in a new paragraph, state another factor and how it could be reduced. There are six marks, so three factors are needed.

Explore

There were several energy transfers as the trolley rolled down the ramp and came to a stop. At the top of the ramp, it had a store of gravitational potential energy. When this was released, it was transferred to the kinetic energy of the trolley. In terms of energy transfers, why does the trolley come to a stop?

Revision Guide page 175.

Hint

You need to know the inter-relationship of acceleration, change in velocity and time taken.

LEARN IT!

Uniformly means at a constant rate.

Maths skills Check that the answer seems reasonable. A car travelling for 20 s is unlikely to cover more than 500 m, or less than 20 m.

Revision Guide page 177.

Explore

Road safety campaigns often focus on reducing the speed of cars. This is because, the faster a car is going, the further it will travel before stopping. If the car does hit something, what are the implications?

---

2. A crash test car of mass 1000 kg is driven at the design-testing centre to examine impact forces. The car starts from rest and accelerates to its final speed.

(a) Write the equation to calculate the acceleration of the car towards the crash barrier in time *t*.

(1 mark

(b) The car accelerates uniformly from 0 m/s to 10 m/s over a time of 20 s. Calculate how far the car will travel.

(3 marks

Distance travelled = …………m

(c) Calculate the momentum of the car as it crashes into the crash barrier.

(2 marks

Momentum = ……………… kg m/s

(d) Which of the following would decrease the momentum in a collision?

(1 mark

☐ **A** decreasing the crumple zones present

☐ **B** increasing the velocity of the vehicle

☐ **C** decreasing the mass of the vehicle

☐ **D** decreasing the time taken to change momentum

(Total for Question 2 = 7 marks

(a) A scientist is working in the countryside to investigate levels of radioactivity on a remote moor. A Geiger–Muller detector is used to measure the count rate. The level recorded is an average of 25 counts per minute.

(i) Give the name of the radiation that the scientist is measuring.

(1 mark)

....

(ii) State two sources of this radiation.

(2 marks)

....

....

....

....

(b) The scientist places a radioactive sample in front of the Geiger–Muller detector and takes some more measurements. The levels recorded now have an average of 200 corrected counts per minute.

(i) Describe what the scientist does to determine the corrected count rate.

(1 mark)

....

....

(ii) Explain why the scientist wears a photographic film badge while he carries out his research.

(2 marks)

....

....

....

....

Revision Guide pages 203–205.

Hint

What kind of radiation is always present, everywhere, every day?

Hint

Some sources of radioactivity are natural, some are man-made. Think about things that are around us all the time.

Practical skills Doing this is like zeroing a top-pan balance before use. There were extra counts that did not come from what was being studied, so the scientist got rid of them.

Practical skills Whenever you do an experiment, you need to think about safety. How could a film badge help make him safer?

Mass affects the ionising properties of radiation. Think about how mass varies with types of radiation.

Explore

The ionising properties are related to the penetrating powers of the different types of radiation. Can you think how?

(c) Describe the nature of alpha, beta and gamma radiation in tern of ionising properties.

(3 mark

....

....

....

....

....

....

(Total for Question 3 = 9 mark

Figure 2 shows the graph of a radio wave.

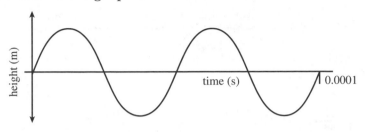

Figure 2

Revision Guide
pages 188–189.

(a) On the graph:

(i) Identify the amplitude of the wave by adding 'A' next to an arrow or marker.

(1 mark)

(ii) Identify the time period of the wave by adding 'T' with arrows or markers.

(1 mark)

(iii) Determine the time period of the wave.

(1 mark)

(b) Determine the frequency of the wave shown in the diagram.

(2 marks)

Frequency =……….……… Hz

(c) Write the equation linking wave speed, wavelength and time period.

(1 mark)

....

(Total for Question 4 = 6 marks)

Hint

How many time periods are shown on the diagram?

LEARN IT!

$$period = \frac{1}{frequency}$$

🔍 **Explore**

Radio waves travel through a vacuum at the speed of light. How might you be able to set up an experiment to directly measure the speed of a radio wave?

LEARN IT!

wave speed = frequency × wavelength

Revision Guide
pages 194 and
196–197.

5. Figure 3 shows part of the electromagnetic spectrum.

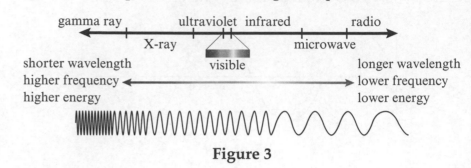

Figure 3

(a) State one use for each of the following waves:

(i) microwaves

(1 mark)

....

(ii) ultraviolet

(1 mark)

....

(iii) gamma rays

(1 mark)

....

(b) Explain which of the waves in (a) is the most damaging to body cells.

(2 marks)

....

....

....

....

Hint

Do not write just 'microwaves' because this is just repeating the question.

Hint

Think about at which end of the spectrum the gamma rays are.

Exam alert

Remember you need to write why the wave is the most damaging, not just name the type of wave.

(c) Which one of the following terms best describes the nature of electromagnetic waves?

(1 mark)

☐ **A** longitudinal

☐ **B** mechanical

☐ **C** seismic

☐ **D** transverse

Hint

Electromagnetic waves can travel through space, which is a vacuum because they do not transfer energy through vibrating particles.

(d) Light from the Sun takes 500 seconds to reach Earth, travelling at 3×10^8 m/s. Calculate the distance of Earth from the Sun. Give your answer in kilometres.

(3 marks)

Maths skills 3×10^8 means 300 000 000. You can think of the 8 as meaning 'move the decimal point 8 places to the right'.

Distance = ……………….. km

(e) Explain why satellites are not used to transmit radio waves but are used to transmit microwaves.

(4 marks)

Explore

Radio signals are divided into ground waves, sky waves and space waves as the wavelength shortens. Find out how these different types of wave got their names.

....

....

....

....

....

....

....

....

(Total for Question 5 = 13 marks)

Revision Guide
pages 182, 183
and 186.

Maths skills Write down the formula. Put in the values from the question. Calculate the answer. Not all the values given will be needed in this part of the question.

Hint

Don't worry about the word 'average'. It is there in case a student starts thinking about the lift having to speed up and slow down. All you have to do is use the total time and total energy and you will get the average power.

Hint

Any mechanical system, similar to a lift, has moving parts that rub together. What happens to them?

6. (a) A lift travels between floors in a building. The lift moves from the ground floor to the fourth floor through a height of 15 m in 20 s. The mass of the lift is 750 kg.

   (i) Calculate how much energy, in joules (J), the lift gains in moving from the ground floor to the fourth floor. Take g to be 10 N/kg.

   (2 marks

   Energy gained, ΔGPE = ...

   (ii) Calculate the average power, in watts (W), that the lift exerts in moving the mass of 750 kg to the fourth floor.

   (2 marks

   Power = ... V

   (b) As the lift moves upwards, not all the energy supplied is usefully transferred. Suggest one way in which energy is not usefully transferred.

   (1 mark

   ....

(c) Calculate the kinetic energy (KE), in J, of the lift when it is moving from the ground floor to the fourth floor.

(4 marks)

Maths skills In the formula, only the speed is squared.

Kinetic energy = ... J

(d) Explain why this mechanical process could be described as wasteful.

Give an example of wasted energy in this process.

(3 marks)

....
....
....
....
....
....

(Total for Question 6 = 11 marks)

TOTAL FOR PAPER = 60

Explore

Whenever a movement is opposed there is energy transferred. Often this energy is wasted. What is the movement and what opposes it when an electrical wire heats up?

Combined Science
Paper 6: Physics 2

Time allowed: 1 hour 10 minutes

Answer ALL questions. Write your answers in the spaces provided.

1. (a) A kettle is rated at 2000 W and designed to operate on a
        230 V mains supply. Calculate the charge moved in the kettle in
        1 second.

        (2 marks

Revision Guide
page 222.

Hint

Remember that W is
the same as J/s.

Charge =......... C

    (b) Explain what happens to the energy in various parts of the
        system when the kettle is switched on.

        (3 marks

Hint

Consider the energy
that is transferred into
and out of the heater,
the water, and the
surroundings.

....
....
....
....
....
....

(c) Draw an energy transfer diagram to illustrate the energy transferred inside the kettle after it has been switched on.

(3 marks)

(d) Describe how energy is not transferred usefully while boiling water in the kettle.

(2 marks)

....

....

(Total for Question 1 = 10 marks)

Revision Guide
page 234.

2. (a) The diagram in Figure 1 shows a wire passing through a card.

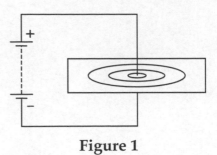

Figure 1

A compass is positioned at various places on the card to determine the direction of the magnetic field round the wire. Explain whether the magnetic field is clockwise or anticlockwise.

(3 marks

....

....

....

....

....

....

Hint

Use the right-hand corkscrew rule.

Watch out!

A solenoid is similar to a bar magnet, but the field lines are inside the coil as well.

(b) (i) The wire is now turned into a solenoid. Draw the new magnetic field that this produces.

(4 marks

Hint

Make sure your diagram is the correct shape and the distance between the lines of flux are correct both inside the coil and outside. You need to show both sides of the electromagnet.

(ii) Suggest a use for this device.

(1 mark)

....

(c) A 0.75 m length of wire carrying a current of 3 A is placed
between two magnets at right angles to the field of 0.5 T.
Calculate the force experienced by the wire. Give the unit.

(3 marks)

Force = ...

(Total for Question 2 = 11 marks)

Hint

Consider what an
electromagnet can
do that a permanent
magnet cannot.

Explore

Work out what
direction the force
would be in. How could
the size of the force
be increased?

Revision Guide
pages 229 and
243.

Maths skills Make sure that you convert the units at the start, for example seconds rather than minutes, metres rather than centimetres, volts rather than kilovolts; kilograms are the one exception.

LEARN IT!

Change in heat energy = mass × specific heat capacity × change in temperature

Hint

If you can't work out part (a), just put a guess down and then use that so that you can still get marks for part (b).

Hint

Think about where some of the heat energy will go.

3. An electrical heater supplies electrical energy to a copper block of mass 2000 g at 12 V with a current of 12 A for 2 minutes.

(a) Calculate the energy supplied to the heater. State the unit.

(3 marks

Energy supplied = ...

(b) Calculate the temperature rise for the block of copper when supplied with the energy from (a) (your answer). The specific heat capacity of copper is 385 J/kg K. State the unit.

(3 marks

Temperature rise = ...

(c) Suggest why the actual temperature rise may be lower than the predicted value.

(1 mar

....

....

(d) (i) Give one way to reduce unwanted energy transfer in the
heating of a metal block.

(1 mark)

Hint

What *do* you do when
you go outside in
the cold and want to
reduce your heat loss?

....

(ii) Give an example of a suitable material that could be used.

(1 mark)

Explore

Consider how you
would design an
experiment to test
which material was
best. What equipment
would you use? What
would you change and
what would you keep
the same?

....

(Total for Question 3 = 9 marks)

Revision Guide
page 221.

Hint

If they are hovering, there is no unbalanced force acting on them.

Hint

Identify which force has been dramatically reduced by turning off the fan, and then make its arrow a lot shorter.

4. Indoor skydivers use a vertical wind tunnel. Moving air travels upwards and keeps a skydiver at a constant height inside the tunnel.

(a) (i) Draw a labelled free body diagram to show the vertical forces acting on a skydiver hovering in a vertical wind tunnel.

(2 marks

(ii) When the wind tunnel is turned off, the skydiver moves towards the ground. Draw a labelled free body diagram to show the vertical forces acting on the skydiver as this happens.

(2 marks

(b) The cyclist shown in Figure 2 is accelerating downhill on a bicycle by pushing on the pedals.

Figure 2

(i)   Identify the force pairs acting on the cyclist and bicycle.

(2 marks)

....

....

....

....

(ii) Sketch a labelled free body diagram to show how these forces are acting on the cyclist and bicycle.

(2 marks)

Hint

Identify means 'name' in this context.

Watch out!

Gravity acts straight down, not diagonally down the slope.

Explore

Some bicycles power their lights using a dynamo attached to a wheel. How would the speed of the bicycle affect the brightness of the lights? What difference would the cyclist notice when the lights were switched on?

(c) Explain how the bicycle transfers energy to the surroundings. Suggest one way in which these transfers can be reduced.

(2 marks

....

....

....

....

(Total for Question 4 = 10 marks

Figure 3 is a circuit diagram that shows three identical lamps and one cell.

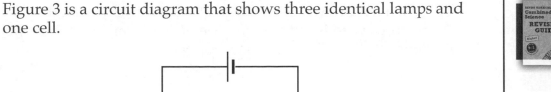

Figure 3

(a) The cell provides 1.5 V. State the potential difference across each lamp.

(1 mark)

....

(b) Figure 4 shows a circuit to test a thermistor.

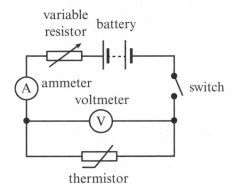

Figure 4

(i) Describe how resistance changes in a thermistor.

(3 marks)

....

....

....

(ii) Give a use for a thermistor in a domestic circuit.

(1 mark)

....

Revision Guide
pages 223, 224 and 239.

LEARN IT!

Potential difference is the difference in potential between two points.

Hint

There is 1.5 V between the right and left sides of the circuit. Consider how that divides up between the lamps.

Hint

As a thermistor gains heat energy, more electrons are able to flow in it. Think how that will affect the current, and thus what must have happened to the resistance.

Hint

Think of something where temperature controls what happens.

(c) Give a reason why the voltage of the electricity from the National Grid is reduced for domestic use, and state how this is done.

(2 marks

....

....

....

(d) (i) Calculate the current in the secondary coil of a step-down transformer, where $V_p = 4600$ V, $I_p = 5$ A and $V_s = 230$ V.

(2 marks

Current = ... /

(ii) State the assumption made when calculating the power of . transformer.

(1 mark

....

(Total for Question 5 = 10 marks

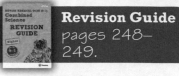

Revision Guide
pages 248–
249.

Two students carry out an experiment to investigate the linear elastic distortion of a thin spring. They add weights to a spring but can find only five weights: one of 0.1 N, one of 0.5 N and three of 1 N. They then measure the final extension. When the spring is unloaded the students find that the spring has stretched.

Practical skills Think about what other equipment you could use, and what other measurements you could take.

(a) Suggest two ways of improving the experiment.

(2 marks)

....

....

....

(b) The table in Figure 5 shows results for the loading of a 32-mm spring.

Hint

Spot the pattern in each column. Then work out the missing numbers.

Weight (N)	Length of spring (mm)
0	32
0.1	
	40
0.3	
0.4	48
	52
0.6	56

Figure 5

Complete the missing values in the table.

(2 marks)

Hint

In this graph, the dependent variable is plotted on the *x*-axis, rather than the *y*-axis as is usual. This is because it makes the gradient equal to the spring constant, so it is more convenient than having to find the reciprocal (1/gradient).

Explore

How could you use the spring and this graph to find out the weight of an object that is less than 0.6 N?

*(c) The students used their results to produce Figure 6. Explain how the graph illustrates linear elastic distortion and how the graph could be improved. Explain how you could extend the experiment to find out the force which makes the spring change shape permanently. You should refer to the graph in your answer

(6 marks

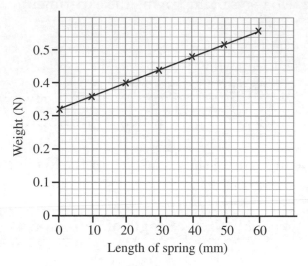

Figure 6

....

....

....

....

....

....

....

....

....

....

....

....

....

....

....

....

....

....

....

(Total for Question 6 = 10 marks

TOTAL FOR PAPER = 60

Combined Science
Paper 1: Biology 1

Time allowed: 1 hour 10 minutes

Answer ALL questions. Write your answers in the spaces provided.

1. Catalase is an enzyme found in many different tissues in plants and animals. It speeds up the breakdown of hydrogen peroxide:

hydrogen peroxide → water + oxygen

A group of students wanted to design an experiment to investigate the amount of catalase in different plant and animal tissues. They knew that when the reaction takes place in a test tube, the oxygen gas given off produces foam. They decided that they could measure the height of the foam in the test tube and use this to estimate the amount of catalase in the different types of tissue.

The group was provided with hydrogen peroxide solution, test tubes and five different plant tissues.

(a) Devise a plan, using the supplied solution and apparatus, to compare the amount of enzyme in different tissues.

(3 marks)

They could add hydrogen peroxide to each test tube ✓ and add different plant tissue to each tube. ✓

Then they could measure the height of the foam after a period of time, for example 30 seconds, but they must use the same length of time for each treatment. ✓

> **Alternative answers:**
> You could also suggest the following in any order:
> - Use the same amount / mass of plant tissue.
> - Use the same volume of hydrogen peroxide solution.

(b) State **two** variables that the students should control in the investigation.

(2 marks)

The students should keep the temperature constant ✓ and use the same volume or concentration of hydrogen peroxide. ✓

> **Alternative answers:**
> You could also suggest the following in any order:
> - Use the same size / mass / amount of tissue each time.
> - Grind / liquidise tissues so that they have the same surface area.
> - Use a buffer to maintain pH.
> - Equilibrate all solutions using a water bath.

(c) Suggest one improvement that the students could make that would increase the accuracy of their measurement of enzyme activity.

(1 mark)

Collect the gas in a gas syringe to measure its volume. ✓

(Total for Question 1 = 6 marks)

2. In humans there are two types of cell division: mitosis and meiosis. The table in Figure 1 gives several statements about cell division.

Tick one box in each row to show if the statement is true for mitosis only, for meiosis only or for both mitosis and meiosis. The first row has been completed for you.

(4 marks)

Statement	Mitosis only	Meiosis only	Both mitosis and meiosis
Used for growth and replacement of cells	✓		
Used for production of gametes		✓	✓
Before the parent cell divides, each chromosome is copied		✓	✓
Produces genetically identical cells	✓		✓
Halves the chromosome number		✓	✓

Figure 1

(Total for Question 2 = 4 marks)

3. A man has an infection as a result of disease-causing bacteria. He has not been immunised against these bacteria. Figure 2 shows how the number of these bacteria changes after a doctor gives the man a 7-day course of antibiotics.

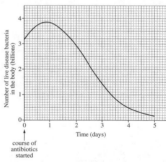

course of antibiotics started

Figure 2

(a) Explain whether the man has a communicable or a non-communicable disease.

(2 marks)

The man has a communicable disease ✓ because it is caused by a bacterium or a pathogen. ✓

(b) The man started feeling better on day 3. Calculate the percentage decrease in the number of live, disease-causing microorganisms between the start of the course of antibiotics and the time that the man started to feel better. Give your answer to one decimal place.

(2 marks)

$$\frac{3.2 - 1.4}{3.2} \times 100 = 56.25\% \quad \checkmark$$

.... 56.3% $\checkmark$ ....

(c) The doctor suspected that the disease was caused by a bacterium not a virus. Use the information in the graph to explain why the doctor was correct.

(3 marks)

After the course of antibiotics was started, the number of bacteria decreased $\checkmark$ and the man felt better. $\checkmark$ Antibiotics do not kill viruses. If the man had been infected with a virus he would not have felt better. $\checkmark$

(d) Figure 3 shows the results of two studies into the effect of alcohol consumption on the risk of developing liver disease. One group (solid line) consisted only of men and the other group (dotted line) consisted only of women.

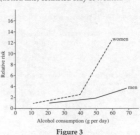

Figure 3

State and explain the relationship between alcohol consumption and relative risk of liver disease for men.

(3 marks)

There is a positive correlation between alcohol consumption and risk of liver disease (as alcohol consumption increases, risk of liver disease also increases). $\checkmark$ The risk increases much more with alcohol consumption greater than 50 g/day $\checkmark$ because ethanol is poisonous, particularly to liver cells. $\checkmark$

(Total for Question 3 = 10 marks)

4. (a) Factor VIII is a blood-clotting factor used to treat people with haemophilia. It is now produced in genetically modified bacteria.

(i) The factor VIII gene was obtained from human DNA. State the type of enzyme used to cut the factor VIII gene out of the human DNA.

(1 mark)

restriction endonuclease $\checkmark$

(ii) The table in Figure 4 shows the processes involved in preparing the genetically modified bacteria, but they are not in the correct order. Complete the table by putting a number in each box to show the correct order. The first one has been completed for you.

(2 marks)

All correct = 2 marks, 1 mistake = 1 mark. You will get 0 marks if you make 2 or more mistakes.

Process	Order
A bacterial plasmid is cut open and mixed with the fragments containing the factor VIII gene	2
DNA fragments containing the factor VIII gene are prepared	1
DNA ligase joins the sticky ends	3
The recombinant plasmid is grown in bacteria to make many copies	5
The complementary bases on the sticky ends pair up	4

Figure 4

 $\checkmark\checkmark$

(iii) Explain the importance of sticky ends and DNA ligase in this process.

(3 marks)

If the same restriction enzyme is used to make the fragment and cut the plasmid, $\checkmark$ the sticky ends will match $\checkmark$ and DNA ligase can be used to make a complete recombinant plasmid. $\checkmark$

(b) Cystic fibrosis is an inherited disease caused by a mutated allele for the CFTR protein found in lungs and other tissues. A couple, neither of whom had cystic fibrosis, came from families that both had a history of the disease. The couple were concerned that they might have children who were affected. They underwent genetic testing and were found to be heterozygous for the cystic fibrosis gene.

(i) Using F for the normal allele and f for the mutated allele, state the genotype of both parents.

(1 mark)

Ff (and Ff) $\checkmark$

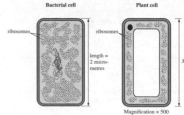

(ii) Predict the percentage probability of the couple's children having cystic fibrosis. Use the Punnett square.

(2 marks)

		Mother's gametes	
		F	f
Father's	F	FF	Ff
gametes	f	Ff	ff

✔

percentage probability of having a child with cystic fibrosis = 25% ✔

(c) Two proteins, DAZL and PRDM14, are involved in the development of sperm cells. Mutations in these genes have been associated with an increased risk of developing testicular cancer. Almost 100% of all testicular cancers can be completely cured if diagnosed early.

Explain how the Human Genome Project has made it possible to improve early diagnosis of diseases, such as testicular cancer, in men with a family history of testicular cancer.

(3 marks)

Being able to determine the base sequence of an individual ✔ means that doctors know if that individual has an increased risk of testicular cancer, ✔ so he can be monitored more closely and diagnosed earlier. ✔

(Total for Question 4 = 12 marks)

9

---

5. Figure 5 shows a bacterial cell and a plant cell.

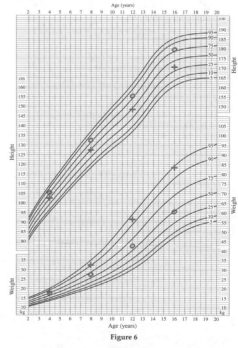

Figure 5

(a) (i) Both types of cell contain ribosomes. State the function of a ribosome.

(1 mark)

makes or synthesises proteins ✔

(ii) The plant cell contains mitochondria but the bacterial cell does not. State **two** other ways in which the plant cell differs from the bacterial cell.

(2 marks)

Plant cells have vacuoles ✔ and chloroplasts. ✔

10

(b) Although the cells are drawn the same size, the magnifications are different. The actual length of the bacterial cell is 2 micrometres.

Calculate the actual length, X, of the plant cell. Give your answer in micrometres in standard form and to one decimal place. Show your working.

(3 marks)

$$\text{magnification} = \frac{\text{image size}}{\text{real size}}$$

$$\text{real size} = \frac{\text{image size}}{\text{magnification}}$$

✔

$$\frac{53}{500} = 0.106 \text{ mm} ✔ \text{ or } 1.1 \times 10^2 \text{ micrometres} ✔$$

(Total for Question 5 = 6 marks)

11

---

6. Figure 6 shows a percentile chart developed by the US government to monitor the growth of males between the ages of 2 and 20 years. It can be used to monitor both weight and height.

Figure 6

(a) Describe how a doctor or nurse could use this chart to monitor the growth of a boy from the age of 2 years to 16 years.

(3 marks)

Measure weight and height ✔ every year or at regular intervals ✔ and plot the results on the chart. ✔

12

81

(b) The table in Figure 7 shows the weight and height records of two boys, A and B, from the ages of 4 to 16.

Age (years)	Height (cm)		Weight (kg)	
	Boy A	Boy B	Boy A	Boy B
4	102	105	18	17
8	127	132	32	27
12	148	155	56	42
16	170	179	83	60

Figure 7

(i) Plot the height and weight of both boys on the chart on page 12. Use '+' for Boy A and 'o' for Boy B.

(4 marks)

> There is 1 mark per set of points correctly plotted as shown in Figure 6.

(ii) Use your chart to suggest what conclusions could be made about the development of the two boys.

(4 marks)

Boy A: is of average or below average height ✓ but in the upper range for weight so is overweight. ✓

Boy B: is of above average height ✓ and average weight so is possibly underweight for his height. ✓

(Total for Question 6 = 11 marks)

13

---

7. Figure 8 shows the neurones and other parts of the body involved in the response to touching a sharp object.

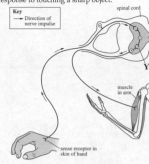

Figure 8

(a) Identify which of the following describes the correct sequence of events after touching a sharp object.

(1 mark)

☐ A sensory receptor → sensory neurone → motor neurone → relay neurone

☐ B sensory receptor → muscle → motor neurone → relay neurone

☐ C sensory receptor → relay neurone → sensory neurone → motor neurone

☒ D sensory receptor → sensory neurone → relay neurone → motor neurone ✓

14

(b) (i) State the name of the structure labelled Y on the diagram.

(1 mark)

synapse ✓

(ii) Describe the events occurring at point Y that allow the impulse to be passed on from one neurone to the next.

(3 marks)

Nerve impulse reaches the axon terminal. ✓
Neurotransmitter substance is released into the gap. ✓
This is detected by the next neurone, ✓ generating a new impulse.

15

---

*(c) Explain how stem cell therapy could be used in the future to treat injuries in the body, such as spinal cord injury. In your answer, you should discuss the sources of stem cells as well as the ethical implications.

(6 marks)

Stem cells are unspecialised cells, which can divide and produce differentiated cells. Stem cells can be obtained from embryos when they are called embryonic stem cells or if they are from the patient they are called adult stem cells.

Embryonic stem cells are taken from embryos at a very early stage of division; they can be used to repair damaged tissue, such as nervous tissue in the spinal cord. They are easy to extract from embryos and can produce any type of cell, including nerve cells. The patient would receive the nervous tissue as a transplant into the spinal cord. However, embryos are destroyed in this process and some people think embryos have a right to life. There is also a danger of rejection because the transplanted tissue is seen as foreign and could be attacked by the patient's immune system.

If adult stem cells are used, they do not require destruction of embryos and will not be rejected (if taken from the person to be treated). However, the types of cells into which adult stem cells will differentiate are limited, and so may not be suitable for treating damaged nerve tissue in the spinal cord. Stem cell therapy may also increase the risk of cancer.

(Total for Question 7 = 11 marks)

TOTAL FOR PAPER = 60 MARKS

16

Combined Science
Paper 2: Biology

Time allowed: 1 hour 10 minutes

Answer ALL questions. Write your answers in the spaces provided.

1. (a) A student carried out an investigation into osmosis in potato pieces. The student cut five pieces of potato, weighed them and then placed them into different concentrations of salt solution. After one hour the student removed the potato pieces from the salt solution and weighed them again. The student's results are shown in the table in Figure 1.

Concentration of salt solution (mol dm^{-3})	Initial mass of potato (g)	Final mass of potato (g)	Percentage change in mass (%)
0.0	5.2	5.4	$\frac{5.4 - 5.2}{5.2} \times 100 = 3.8$ 3.8% increase
0.25	5.6	5.6	$\frac{5.6 - 5.6}{5.6} \times 100 = 0.0$ 0.0% increase
0.5	5.6	5.4	$\frac{5.4 - 5.6}{5.6} \times 100 = -3.6$ 3.6% decrease
1.0	5.0	4.6	$\frac{4.6 - 5.0}{5.0} \times 100 = -8.0$ 8.0% decrease
1.5	5.2	4.2	$\frac{4.2 - 5.2}{5.2} \times 100 = -19.2$ 19.2% decrease

Figure 1

(i) Complete the table by calculating the percentage change in mass of the potato pieces. Give your answers to 1 decimal place.

(3 marks)

All correct = 3 marks,
4 correct = 2 marks,
3 correct = 1 mark.
0 marks if 2 or fewer correct.

Alternative answers:
You could also say:
• use the same surface area of potato pieces
• blot the pieces dry before measuring mass
• keep all tubes at the same temperature
• cover tubes to prevent solution evaporating.

(ii) Give one step the student should take to increase the accuracy and repeatability of the measurements.

(1 mark)

Use the same shape of potato piece. ✔

(iii) Use your results from part (i) to estimate the solute concentration of the potato cells.

(1 mark)

0.25 mol dm^{-3} ✔

(b) Figure 2 shows the part of the lung where gas exchange takes place.

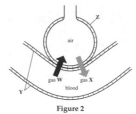

Figure 2

(i) State the names of the structures labelled **Y** and **Z** in the diagram.

(2 marks)

Structure Y is the capillary wall. ✔

Structure Z is the wall of the alveolus. ✔

(ii) Which one of the following methods describes how gases W and X move in the directions shown?

(1 mark)

☒ A diffusion ✔
☐ B osmosis
☐ C breathing
☐ D respiration

(iii) State the name of gas X.

(1 mark)

carbon dioxide ✔

(c) A scientist recently estimated that the average human lung has 480 million alveoli and that 1 million alveoli have a surface area of 0.15 m^2.

Calculate the total surface area of a human lung.

(2 marks)

480×0.15 ✔ $= 72$ m^2 ✔

(Total for Question 1 = 11 marks)

---

2. Figure 3 shows the heart rate of an adult male over a 24-hour period.

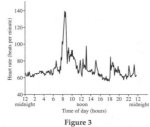

Figure 3

(a) (i) Use the graph to estimate this person's resting heart rate.

(1 mark)

60 beats per minute ✔

(ii) The man attended a one hour spinning (indoor cycling) class during the day. Use the graph to estimate the start time of the class.

(1 mark)

7.30–8.00 am ✔

(iii) About an hour before the class started the man walked uphill to the gym where the class was held. He then rested until the class started.

Give one piece of evidence from the trace that supports this.

(1 mark)

Heart rate increases to a peak of about 80 and then falls again shortly before the main peak. ✔

(iv) The man noticed that his heart rate remained higher than normal for some time after the end of the class.

Explain why his heart rate remained high.

(2 marks)

The man's heart rate remained high because extra oxygen is needed to replace the oxygen used in the exercise ✔ and to oxidise the lactic acid produced. ✔

(b) (i) The table in Figure 4 shows the stroke volume and heart rate for two people measured while they were at rest.

Complete the table by calculating the cardiac output for each person. Include the units for cardiac output.

(3 marks)

	Stroke volume (cm³)	Heart rate (beats/min)	Cardiac output	Units
Person A	95	52	4940	cm³/min
Person B	58	72	4176	cm³/min

Figure 4

Person A = 95 × 52 = 4940 ✓

Person B = 58 × 72 = 4176 ✓

Units for cardiac output = cm³/min ✓

(ii) One of these people was a trained athlete, the other was untrained. Suggest and explain which is the trained athlete.

(2 marks)

Person A is the trained athlete ✓ because he or she had the higher cardiac output. ✓

Alternative answer: You could also give the reasons:

• higher stroke volume

• lower heart rate.

(Total for Question 2 = 10 marks)

21

22

3. (a) The term assisted reproductive therapy (ART) covers a number of treatments to help couples who are having difficulty conceiving a child. Various hormones and drugs are used in ART. One such hormone is FSH.

(i) State where FSH is produced.

(1 mark)

pituitary gland ✓

(ii) Describe the effect of FSH on the ovary.

(1 mark)

It stimulates growth and maturation of a follicle. ✓

(b) The drug clomifene can be used to treat women who have difficulty conceiving.

(i) Explain how clomifene can help such women conceive.

(2 marks)

Clomifene stimulates production of FSH and LH, ✓ so women who don't normally produce enough of these hormones will ovulate normally with the help of clomifene. ✓

(ii) Explain why clomifene is used to stimulate ovulation in women undergoing IVF, even if they ovulate naturally.

(2 marks)

Clomifene stimulates the maturation of many follicles or eggs at the same time, ✓ so that there are more eggs available for fertilisation in vitro (IVF). ✓

(Total for Question 3 = 6 marks)

4. Adrenalin and noradrenalin are chemically similar molecules. However, adrenalin is a hormone and noradrenalin is a neurotransmitter.

(a) State the organ where adrenalin is produced.

(1 mark)

adrenal gland ✓

(b) Describe how adrenalin reaches its target organs.

(2 marks)

Adrenalin is secreted into the blood ✓ and transported around the body in the blood. ✓

(c) Describe **two** ways in which hormonal communication is different to nervous communication.

(2 marks)

Hormones are secreted into the blood, whereas nerve impulses travel along nerves. ✓
Hormones have a long-lived effect, whereas nerves have a short-term effect. ✓

Alternative answers: You could also suggest the differences.

• Nerve impulses work quickly; hormones take longer to work.

• Hormones can have effects on many different parts of the body; nerves act on specific organs.

(d) Adrenalin causes muscle cells to convert glycogen to glucose.

(i) State the name of one other hormone that has the same effect.

(1 mark)

glucagon ✓

(ii) State the name of the disease caused by the body not being able to regulate the concentration of glucose in the blood.

(1 mark)

diabetes ✓

(Total for Question 4 = 7 marks)

23

24

5. An epiphyte is a plant that grows harmlessly on another plant, and obtains its water and nutrients from the air, rain and debris that accumulate around it.

(a) Mistletoe is a parasitic plant. Explain how a parasite differs from an epiphyte.

(3 marks)

Mistletoe grows roots into the tree ✓ and absorbs water
and nutrients from the host ✓ which can damage the host
tree, reducing its growth. ✓

(b) Nitrogen-fixing bacteria grow in the root nodules of legumes. Explain why nitrogen-fixing bacteria are considered to be mutualists rather than parasites.

(3 marks)

Nitrogen-fixing bacteria are protected and get food from the
plant. ✓ The legume gets the nitrogen compounds that it
needs from the bacteria, ✓ so each organism benefits. ✓

(Total for Question 5 = 6 marks)

25

---

6. A group of students were undertaking a survey of an area of land alongside a path that crossed a field and entered a piece of woodland.

(a) (i) State **two** abiotic factors that might influence the distribution of plant species in the woodland.

(2 marks)

light intensity ✓
water availability ✓

(ii) State **two** biotic factors that might influence the distribution of plant species next to the path in the field.

(2 marks)

predation or grazing by animals ✓
competition for light and space ✓

26

---

*(b) Describe how the students should survey the abundance of different plant species growing alongside the path from the field and into the wood.

(6 marks)

To survey the abundance of different plant species growing
alongside the path from the field and into the wood, the
students should use a belt transect. They should use a tape
measure to place quadrats at regular intervals alongside the
path.

In each quadrat they should count the number of each different
plant species or calculate the percentage cover of each
different plant species.

At each quadrat position, they should record abiotic factors
(temperature, light intensity, etc.) and record biotic factors,
e.g. shade from tree, animals.

They could present the results as a table or a graph.

(Total for Question 6 = 10 marks)

27

---

7. (a) Figure 5 shows a specialised type of plant tissue.

Figure 5

(i) Which specialised plant tissue is shown in Figure 5?

(1 mark)

☐ A xylem
☒ B phloem ✓
☐ C mesophyll
☐ D root hair

(ii) Identify the parts labelled E and F.

(2 marks)

E is a _sieve tube_ ✓

F is a _sieve plate_ ✓

(iii) Explain why the companion cell contains large numbers of mitochondria.

(3 marks)

Mitochondria supply energy from respiration, ✓ which is
used to move sucrose in and out of the companion cell ✓ by
active transport. ✓

28

85

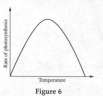

Paper 2 Answers

(b) (i) Temperature can be a limiting factor in photosynthesis. State **one** other factor that can limit the rate of photosynthesis.

(1 mark)

light intensity ✓

(ii) Figure 6 shows how the rate of photosynthesis changes as temperature is increased. Explain how the rate of photosynthesis changes as the temperature is increased.

(3 marks)

Figure 6

The rate of photosynthesis increases and then decreases. ✓
Increasing the temperature increases the rate of enzyme
reactions, ✓ but only up to a certain point, because very high
temperatures denature enzymes so at these higher
temperatures the rate slows down. ✓

(Total for Question 7 = 10 marks)

TOTAL FOR PAPER = 60 MARKS

29

Combined Science
Paper 3: Chemistry 1

Time allowed: 1 hour 10 minutes

Answer ALL questions. Write your answers in the spaces provided.

1. (a) The table in Figure 1 gives the numbers of protons, neutrons and electrons in five different particles (**V**, **W**, **X**, **Y** and **Z**).

Particle	Protons	Neutrons	Electrons
V	8	8	8
W	11	12	11
X	13	14	10
Y	15	16	18
Z	18	22	18

Figure 1

(i) Which particle is a positively charged **ion**?

(1 mark)

- ☐ A particle W
- ☒ B particle X ✔
- ☐ C particle Y
- ☐ D particle Z

(ii) Which particles are **atoms** of non-metals?

(1 mark)

- ☐ A particles V and W
- ☐ B particles W and X
- ☐ C particles X and Y
- ☒ D particles V and Z ✔

(b) A sample of neon consists of 90.5% $^{20}_{10}$Ne and 9.5% $^{22}_{10}$Ne.

(i) Describe, in terms of subatomic particles, why these are isotopes of the same element.

(4 marks)

Isotopes of an element contain the same number of protons ✔ but different numbers of neutrons. ✔ Both these atoms have 10 protons ✔ but one has 10 neutrons and the other has 12 neutrons. ✔

(ii) Calculate the relative atomic mass, A_r, of this sample of neon. Give your answer to one decimal place.

(3 marks)

$(90.5 \times 20) + (9.5 \times 22)$

$= 2019$ ✔

$A_r = \dfrac{2019}{100}$

$= 20.19$ ✔

Relative atomic mass = 20.2 ✔

(Total for Question 1 = 9 marks)

2. This question is about electrons and the periodic table.

(a) Complete the diagram below to show the electronic configuration of phosphorus, P.

(1 mark)

  ✔

(b) State, in terms of their electronic configurations, why fluorine and chlorine are placed in group 7.

(1 mark)

Atoms of both elements have seven electrons in their outer shell. ✔

(c) Explain, in terms of their electronic configurations, why magnesium is in period 3 but calcium is in period 4.

(2 marks)

Magnesium is in period 3 because its atoms have three occupied shells. ✔
Calcium is in period 4 because its atoms have four occupied shells. ✔

(Total for Question 2 = 4 marks)

3. The table in Figure 2 gives the formulae of three ions.

Name of ion	Formula of ion
aluminium	Al^{3+}
hydroxide	OH^-
sulfate	SO_4^{2-}

Figure 2

(a) Which of these is the correct formula for aluminium sulfate?

(1 mark)

- ☐ A Al_2SO_4
- ☐ B $Al_3(SO_4)_2$
- ☒ C $Al_2(SO_4)_3$ ✔
- ☐ D Al_2SO_4

(b) The atomic number of fluorine is 9 and its mass number is 19. Calculate the numbers of protons, neutrons and electrons in a fluoride ion, F^-.

(3 marks)

Protons .... 9 ✔

Neutrons .... 19 − 9 = 10 ✔

Electrons .... 9 + 1 = 10 ✔

(c) Aluminium sulfate is soluble in water. It is used in the treatment of water for drinking.

(i) A solution of aluminium sulfate is formed by dissolving 35 g of aluminium sulfate in 250 cm³ of water.

Calculate the concentration, in g dm⁻³, of this solution.
(2 marks)

Alternative answer: You could also show your working out like this:

- concentration =
$\frac{35}{250} \times 1000$ ✓ =

140 ✓ g dm⁻³

Volume of water $= \dfrac{250}{1000} = 0.25\ dm^3$

Concentration $= \dfrac{35}{0.25}$ ✓

$= 140\ g\ dm^{-3}$

✓

(ii) A precipitate of aluminium hydroxide is produced during the treatment of water. This sticky solid traps other small pieces of insoluble solid, so they sink to the bottom of the water treatment tank.

Write a balanced ionic equation for the reaction between aluminium ions and hydroxide ions in solution to form aluminium hydroxide. Include state symbols.
(3 marks)

$Al^{3+}(aq) + 3OH^-(aq) \rightarrow Al(OH)_3(s)$

formulae ✓
balanced ✓
state symbols ✓

(Total for Question 3 = 9 marks)

---

4. Air is a mixture of gases, including nitrogen, oxygen and carbon dioxide.

(a) Why does nitrogen have a low boiling point?
(1 mark)

☒ **A** There are weak forces of attraction between nitrogen molecules. ✓

☐ **B** There are weak covalent bonds between nitrogen molecules.

☐ **C** There are weak forces of attraction between nitrogen atoms.

☐ **D** There are weak covalent bonds between nitrogen atoms.

(b) Explain how a covalent bond forms.
(2 marks)

A pair of outer electrons ✓ is shared between two atoms. ✓

(c) Draw a dot-and-cross diagram to show a molecule of carbon dioxide, CO_2. Show the outer electrons only.
(2 marks)

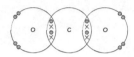

Two bonding pairs of electrons between each O and C ✓

Two non-bonding pairs of electrons on each O atom ✓

(d) Figure 3 shows the structures of diamond and graphite.

diamond   graphite

Figure 3

Explain, in terms of structure and bonding, why diamond has a very high melting point.
(2 marks)

Diamond has a giant covalent structure. ✓ This contains many strong covalent bonds ✓ which need a lot of energy to break.

(Total for Question 4 = 7 marks)

---

5. A student adds magnesium to an excess of dilute hydrochloric acid in an evaporating basin. Magnesium chloride solution and hydrogen gas form. When the reaction is complete, the student carefully evaporates the magnesium chloride solution to dryness. The table in Figure 4 shows her results.

Object	Mass (g)
empty evaporating basin	86.43
evaporating basin with magnesium	87.64
magnesium used	1.21 ✓
evaporating basin with magnesium chloride	91.22
magnesium chloride formed	4.79 ✓

Figure 4

(a) Complete the table to show the mass of magnesium used, and the mass of magnesium chloride formed.
(2 marks)

$87.64 - 86.43 = 1.21$

$91.22 - 86.43 = 4.79$

(b) Use your answers to part (a) to calculate the mass of chlorine present in the magnesium chloride.
(1 mark)

Mass of chlorine

= mass of magnesium chloride – mass of magnesium

$= 4.79 - 1.21$

Mass of chlorine = 3.58 ✓ g

(c) Use your answers to parts (a) and (b) to calculate the **empirical formula** of magnesium chloride.
(Relative atomic masses: Mg = 24, Cl = 35.5)

(3 marks)

	Mg	Cl
mass	1.21	3.58
A_r	24	35.5
$\dfrac{Mass}{A_r}$	$\dfrac{1.21}{24} = 0.05$	$\dfrac{3.58}{35.5} = 0.10$ ✓
simplest ratio	$\dfrac{0.05}{0.05} = 1$	$\dfrac{0.10}{0.05} = 2$ ✓

Empirical formula = ...$MgCl_2$.......... ✓

(Total for Question 5 = 6 marks)

---

6. This question is about drinking water.

(a) Which of these describes clean drinking water?

(1 mark)

- ☐ **A** a pure substance
- ☐ **B** a simple molecular compound
- ☒ **C** a mixture of substances ✓
- ☐ **D** not potable

(b) Drinking water can be made by the simple distillation of seawater.

(i) Describe, in terms of the arrangement and relative energy of water particles, what happens when water boils.

(2 marks)

As the water is heated, the water particles gain energy and move faster. ✓ As it boils, the particles escape from the water and move much further apart. ✓

(ii) Explain why distilled water, rather than tap water, is suitable for use in chemical analysis.

(2 marks)

Tap water contains dissolved salts, which would react with the substances used. ✓ Distilled water does not contain dissolved salts, so it does not interfere with the chemical analysis. ✓

(c) Fresh water can be made safe for drinking at a water treatment plant. Sedimentation is needed to allow small particles to settle out. Filtration and chlorination are also needed.

(i) Describe why filtration is needed.

(1 mark)

Filtration removes very small solid particles that were not removed by sedimentation. ✓

(ii) Explain why chlorination is needed.

(2 marks)

Chlorination involves adding chlorine to the water. ✓ This kills harmful bacteria that might cause disease. ✓

(Total for Question 6 = 8 marks)

---

7. This question is about making salts.

(a) Which row in the table correctly identifies a soluble substance and an insoluble substance?

(1 mark)

	Soluble in water	Insoluble in water
☐ A	silver chloride	lead chloride
☒ B	sodium carbonate	calcium sulfate	✓
☐ C	sodium chloride	calcium chloride
☐ D	barium sulfate	barium nitrate

(b) Predict whether a precipitate will form when sodium hydroxide solution and iron(III) chloride solution are mixed together. Name any precipitate that forms.

(1 mark)

A precipitate of iron(III) hydroxide forms. ✓

(c) Aqueous solutions can be acidic, neutral or alkaline.

(i) State the type of aqueous solution that contains an excess of hydroxide ions, OH⁻(aq).

(1 mark)

an alkaline solution ✓

(ii) An acidic solution, with a pH of 0.70, contains 0.20 mol dm⁻³ of hydrogen ions, H⁺(aq).

Predict the pH of an acidic solution that contains 0.020 mol dm⁻³ of H⁺(aq).

(1 mark)

pH 1.70 ✓

(iii) Explain, in terms of ions, the difference between a strong acid and a weak acid.

(2 marks)

A strong acid is fully dissociated into ions in aqueous solution, ✓ but a weak acid is only partially dissociated into ions. ✓

---

*(d) Plan an experiment to prepare pure, dry, hydrated crystals of copper chloride, $CuCl_2$, from an insoluble copper compound and a suitable dilute acid. In your answer, include the names of suitable reagents and describe any essential stages. You may wish to write a balanced equation to help with your plan.

(6 marks)

Add about 25 cm³ of dilute hydrochloric acid to a beaker. Warm the acid using a water bath filled with hot water from a kettle, or using a Bunsen burner, tripod and gauze mat. Add a spatula of copper oxide powder and stir. This is the equation for the reaction that happens:
$CuO + 2HCl \rightarrow CuCl_2 + H_2O$
Carry on adding copper oxide powder and stirring until some of it is left still unreacted in the beaker. Filter the mixture to remove the excess copper oxide powder. Pour the filtrate into an evaporating basin. Heat it gently to evaporate some of the water to form crystals. Stop heating and let it cool down, so crystals form. Pour away the excess liquid, and dry the crystals with filter paper or in a warm oven.

Alternative answers:
You could use copper carbonate, instead of copper oxide:

- $CuCO_3 + 2HCl \rightarrow CuCl_2 + H_2O + CO_2$

- The evaporating basin could be left aside in a warm place for a few days, instead of heating to evaporate some of the water.

(Total for Question 7 = 12 marks)

8. This question is about electrolysis.

(a) State what is meant by the term **electrolyte**.

(2 marks)

An electrolyte is an ionic compound ✓ in the molten state or dissolved in water. ✓

(b) Copper and chlorine form during the electrolysis of concentrated copper chloride solution. Which row in the table correctly shows what happens at the negative electrode?

(1 mark)

	Product formed	Type of reaction
☒ A	copper	reduction
☐ B	copper	oxidation
☐ C	chlorine	reduction
☐ D	chlorine	oxidation

✓

(c) Aluminium is extracted by the electrolysis of aluminium oxide, dissolved in molten cryolite.

(i) State why aluminium cannot be extracted from aluminium oxide by heating with carbon.

(1 mark)

Aluminium is more reactive than carbon ✓ (so carbon cannot reduce aluminium oxide to aluminium).

Alternative answer:
You could give the reverse argument:
- Carbon is less reactive than aluminium (so it cannot reduce aluminium oxide to aluminium).

(ii) Balance the half equation below for the reaction that occurs at the anode.

(1 mark)

$2 O^{2-} \rightarrow O_2 + 4 e^-$ ✓

(Total for Question 8 = 5 marks)

TOTAL FOR PAPER = 60 MARKS

Combined Science
Paper 4: Chemistry 2

Time: 1 hour 10 minutes

Answer ALL questions. Write your answers in the spaces provided.

1. This question is about the alkali metals, the elements in group 1 of the periodic table.

(a) Which of these shows the typical physical properties of the alkali metals?

(1 mark)

☒ A soft with relatively low melting points ✓

☐ B soft with relatively high melting points

☐ C hard with relatively low melting points

☐ D hard with relatively high melting points

(b) Potassium reacts with water. The reaction produces potassium hydroxide solution, KOH, and hydrogen gas, H_2.

(i) Write the balanced equation for the reaction between potassium and water.

(2 marks)

$2K + 2H_2O \rightarrow 2KOH + H_2$

formulae ✓

balanced ✓

(ii) Describe what is seen when a piece of potassium is added to a trough of water.

(2 marks)

There is very rapid fizzing ✓ and the metal ignites and burns with a lilac flame. ✓

Alternative answers:
You could also write:
- the metal floats
- sparks are given off
- metal dissolves / disappears
- metal moves around rapidly
- there is a small explosion at the end.

(c) The electronic configuration of lithium is 2.1.

(i) Write the electronic configurations of sodium and potassium.

(2 marks)

sodium $\quad$ 2.8.1 ✓

potassium $\quad$ 2.8.8.1 ✓

(ii) Explain the trend in the reactivity of the group 1 metals.

(3 marks)

Reactivity increases down the group. ✓ Going down the group, the atoms get larger so the outer electron gets further from the nucleus. ✓ The force of attraction between the nucleus and the outer electron gets weaker, so the electron is lost more easily. ✓

Alternative answer:
You could write:
- As the atoms get larger the outer electron becomes more shielded.

(Total for Question 1 = 10 marks)

---

2. This question is about the halogens, the elements in group 7 of the periodic table.

(a) Which row in the table correctly shows the colours and physical states of the halogens at room temperature and pressure?

(1 mark)

	Chlorine	Bromine	Iodine
☐ A	pale yellow liquid	red–brown liquid	red–brown solid
☐ B	yellow–green gas	purple liquid	purple-black solid
☒ C	yellow–green gas	red–brown liquid	purple-black solid
☐ D	yellow–green gas	purple liquid	red–brown liquid

✓

(b) Describe the chemical test for chlorine.

(2 marks)

Damp blue litmus paper ✓ turns red, then bleaches white. ✓

Alternative answer:
- Damp starch–iodide paper turns blue–black.

*(c) In aqueous solution, chlorine reacts with sodium iodide, NaI. Sodium chloride solution and iodine solution form:

$$Cl_2 + 2NaI \rightarrow 2NaCl + I_2$$

Explain, in terms of electron gain and loss, why this reaction is a redox reaction. You may include half equations in your answer.
(6 marks)

....

In the reaction, chlorine gains electrons and is reduced to

chloride ions:

$$Cl_2 + 2e^- \rightarrow 2Cl^-$$

At the same time, iodide ions lose electrons and are oxidised to

Alternative answer:
$2I^- - 2e^- \rightarrow I_2$

form iodine:

$$2I^- \rightarrow I_2 + 2e^-$$

It is a redox reaction because these processes of reduction and

oxidation happen together.

....

....

(Total for Question 2 = 9 marks)

---

3. A student investigates the rate of reaction between calcium carbonate (marble chips) and excess dilute hydrochloric acid:

$$CaCO_3(s) + 2HCl(aq) \rightarrow CaCl_2(aq) + H_2O(l) + CO_2(g)$$

(a) Which of these would increase the rate of reaction?
(1 mark)

☐ A adding water to the acid

☐ B increasing the volume of acid

☐ C increasing the size of the marble chips

☒ D using calcium carbonate powder instead of marble chips ✓

(b) The student added 0.50 g of calcium carbonate to 50 cm³ of 0.40 mol dm⁻³ hydrochloric acid. Show, by calculation, that the acid is in excess. (Relative formula mass of $CaCO_3 = 100$)
(4 marks)

$$\text{Amount of } CaCO_3 = \frac{0.50}{100}$$

$$= 0.0050 ✓ \text{ mol}$$

$$\text{Volume of acid} = \frac{50}{1000} = 0.050 \text{ dm}^3$$

$$\text{Amount of } HCl = 0.40 \times 0.050$$

Amount of HCl = ...0.020... ✓ mol

From the equation, 1 mol of $CaCO_3$ reacts with 2 mol of HCl. ✓

So $(2 \times 0.0050) = 0.010$ mol of HCl is needed, but there is

more than this. ✓

Alternative answer:
You could also show your working out for the hydrochloric acid like this:

• Amount = $0.40 \times \dfrac{50}{1000}$

= 0.020

(c) The student measured the volume of carbon dioxide produced until all the calcium carbonate had reacted. Figure 1 shows the results that she obtained at 20 °C.

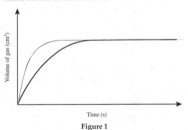

Figure 1

(i) Sketch, on the same axes above, the results that the student would obtain by repeating the experiment at a higher temperature.
(2 marks)

Line drawn to the left of the original, starting at origin and with a similar shape but steeper. ✓

Line becomes horizontal at the same volume as the original. ✓

(ii) Explain, in terms of particles, why increasing the temperature has this effect on the rate of reaction.
(3 marks)

At a higher temperature, the reactant particles have more

energy so they move faster. ✓ They collide more frequently ✓

and more collisions have the activation energy or more. ✓

....

....

....

(Total for Question 3 = 10 marks)

Alternative answers:
You could also write:

• There are more collisions per unit time and

• a greater proportion of collisions is successful.

---

4. Hydrogen peroxide solution decomposes to form water and oxygen:

$$2H_2O_2(aq) \rightarrow 2H_2O(l) + O_2(g)$$

The reaction is exothermic.

(a) Draw and label the reaction profile diagram for this reaction on Figure 2. Label the activation energy.
(3 marks)

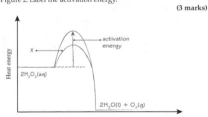

Figure 2

(a) Labelled product line is to the right of the labelled reactant line, and below it. ✓

Upwards curve drawn from reactant line to product line. ✓

Upwards arrow from reactant line to the top of the curve, labelled activation energy. ✓

(b) Manganese dioxide, MnO_2, acts as a catalyst for this reaction.

(i) On the same axes as above, draw the reaction profile for the same reaction in the presence of a catalyst. Label this line with an **X**.
(1 mark)

(b) Upwards curve drawn below the first curve, labelled X. ✓

(ii) Explain, in terms of energy, how a catalyst works.
(2 marks)

A catalyst provides an alternative reaction pathway ✓ with a
lower activation energy. ✓

Alternative answer:
You could also
describe the enzyme
as a biological
catalyst.

(c) If a piece of raw liver is added to hydrogen peroxide solution,
rapid bubbling is observed. Suggest reasons that explain this
observation.
(2 marks)

The raw liver contains an enzyme ✓ that catalyses the
reaction. ✓

(Total for Question 4 = 8 marks)

---

5. Ethene undergoes complete combustion in oxygen to form carbon
dioxide and water as shown in Figure 3:

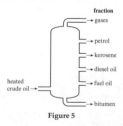

Figure 3

(a) The energies of some bonds are shown in Figure 4. Calculate the
energy change for the complete combustion of 1 mol of ethene.
(4 marks)

Bond	Bond energy (kJ mol⁻¹)
C–H	413
O=O	498
C=O	805
C=C	612
O–H	464

Figure 4

Energy in to break bonds = 612 + (4 × 413) + (3 × 498)

= 3758 kJ mol⁻¹ ✓

Energy out when new bonds form = (4 × 805) + (4 × 464)

= 5076 kJ mol⁻¹ ✓

Energy change = energy in − energy out

= 3758 − 5076

Energy change = ...−1318... kJ mol⁻¹ ✓✓

(b) Explain, in terms of the energy involved in breaking bonds and
making bonds, why this reaction is exothermic.
(2 marks)

More energy is released when bonds form in the products ✓
than is taken in to break bonds in the reactants. ✓

(Total for Question 5 = 6 marks)

---

6. This question is about crude oil.

(a) Which of these statements about crude oil is correct?
(1 mark)

☐ A   It is a renewable resource.

☒ B   It contains molecules with carbon atoms in rings and
chains. ✓

☐ C   It is a complex mixture of carbohydrates.

☐ D   At room temperature, it contains only liquids.

(b) Crude oil is separated into fractions using fractional distillation.
Figure 5 shows an oil-fractionating column and the main
fractions obtained from it.

fraction

→ gases

→ petrol

→ kerosene

→ diesel oil

heated
crude oil →

→ fuel oil

→ bitumen

Figure 5

Identify the fraction which:

(i) has the highest boiling point
(1 mark)

bitumen ✓

(ii) is used as a fuel for aircraft.
(1 mark)

kerosene ✓

(c) State why crude oil may be described as a finite resource.
(1 mark)

Crude oil is made extremely slowly. ✓

(d) Explain how the different substances in crude oil are separated
by fractional distillation.
(4 marks)

Hydrocarbon vapours rise through the fractionating column.
They cool as they rise, and condense at different heights. ✓
The fractions with smaller molecules condense higher up ✓
because they have weaker intermolecular forces, ✓ so their
boiling points are lower. ✓

(Total for Question 6 = 8 marks)

**Alternative answers
to 6(c):** You could
also write that:

• crude oil takes
  millions of years to
  form or

• it is not being made
  any more.

**Alternative answers
to 6(d):** You could
state that:

• The fractionating
  column contains
  a temperature
  gradient, and gets
  cooler towards the
  top.

You could also write
about the reverse
situation, for example:

• fractions with larger
  molecules condense
  lower down

• because they
  have stronger
  intermolecular forces

• so their boiling
  points are higher.

7. This question is about the Earth's atmosphere.

(a) Which of these gases was the most abundant in the Earth's earliest atmosphere?

(1 mark)

☐ A   nitrogen
☐ B   oxygen
☐ C   argon
☒ D   carbon dioxide ✓

(b) Explain how the amount of carbon dioxide in the atmosphere changed over geological time.

(3 marks)

The amount of carbon dioxide decreased over time. ✓ As the
Earth cooled, water vapour in the atmosphere condensed to
form the oceans, and carbon dioxide dissolved in them. ✓
Photosynthesis by plants also used carbon dioxide from the
air. ✓

(c) The combustion of fossil fuels needs oxygen, found in air.

(i) Describe the chemical test for oxygen.

(2 marks)

Light a splint then gently blow it out and place in the gas,
whilst still glowing. The glowing splint ✓ should relight. ✓

(ii) The combustion of fossil fuels releases carbon dioxide into the air. Explain how this gas could cause a change in the temperature of the Earth.

(3 marks)

Carbon dioxide is a greenhouse gas ✓ that contributes to
the greenhouse effect. Carbon dioxide molecules absorb heat
radiated from the Earth's surface, ✓ then release energy in all
directions. This increases the temperature of the Earth. ✓

(Total for Question 7 = 9 marks)

TOTAL FOR PAPER = 60 MARKS

Combined Science
Practice Paper 5: Physics 1

Time allowed: 1 hour 10 minutes

Answer ALL questions. Write your answers in the spaces provided.

1. Robert and Nolly plan to set up an experiment to measure speed. They have a trolley, an inclined ramp, a ruler and a stopwatch.

    (a) Describe a method that the students could use to measure the speed of the trolley using the apparatus above.

    (3 marks)

    Choose a distance to be travelled by the trolley and mark this on the ramp. ✓ Place the trolley at the top of the ramp and let it go. Time how long it takes to cover the marked distance. ✓ Repeat the experiment to reduce the influence of random errors. ✓

    > Both distance and timing should be mentioned for the mark.

    (b) Suggest other apparatus that the students could use to improve the precision of the data collected.

    (2 marks)

    light gates ✓ and data logger ✓

    > **Alternative answer:** You could also suggest:
    > • computer

(c) Robert and Nolly then extend their experiment to investigate the influence of another independent variable. The table in Figure 1 shows data collected by the students.

Height (cm)	Distance (m)	Time (s) ✓	Speed (m/s)
5	1.80	3.2	0.56
10	1.80	2.4	0.75
15	1.80	1.8	1.0
20	1.80	1.4	1.29
25	1.80	1.0	1.8 ✓
30	1.80	0.4	4.5
35	1.80	0.2	9.0

Figure 1

(i) Deduce what the new independent variable might be and add titles for all **three** completed columns in the table.

(1 mark)

height

(ii) Add a fourth column heading, with units, that could be added to the table to help with analysis. Add the **two** missing entries for the fourth column.

(1 mark)

$$\text{speed (m/s)} = \frac{\text{distance (m)}}{\text{time (s)}}$$

$$\text{at 10 s:} \frac{1.80}{2.4} = 0.75$$

$$\text{at 25 s:} \frac{1.80}{1.0} = 1.8$$

*(d) After travelling down the ramp, the trolley comes to a stop by itself. Discuss factors that would have caused the trolley to come to a stop and how these factors could be reduced.

(6 marks)

The trolley comes to a stop by itself because there are resistive forces acting opposite to the motion of the trolley (causing the trolley to stop) – friction and air resistance.

Friction occurs between the wheels and the surface, and between the trolley axles and wheels. Friction could be reduced by using a smoother surface on the ramp, a smoother surface on the wheels and lubricating the axles.

Air resistance could be reduced by making the trolley more aerodynamic and/or reducing the surface area of the front of the trolley.

(Total for Question 1 = 13 marks)

2. A crash test car of mass 1000 kg is driven at the design-testing centre to examine impact forces. The car starts from rest and accelerates to its final speed.

    (a) Write the equation to calculate the acceleration of the car towards the crash barrier in time *t*.

    (1 mark)

    $$a = \frac{v - u}{t} ✓$$

    (b) The car accelerates uniformly from 0 m/s to 10 m/s over a time of 20 s. Calculate how far the car will travel.

    (3 marks)

    $$\text{Average speed} = \frac{10 - 0}{2} = 5 \text{ m/s} ✓$$

    Distance travelled = average speed × time taken

    Distance travelled = 5 m/s × 20 s ✓

    Distance travelled = 100 ✓ m

    (c) Calculate the momentum of the car as it crashes into the crash barrier.

    (2 marks)

    Momentum = mass × velocity

    Momentum = 1000 kg × 10 m/s ✓

    Momentum = 10 000 ✓ kg m/s

    (d) Which of the following would decrease the momentum in a collision?

    (1 mark)

    ☐ A decreasing the crumple zones present
    ☐ B increasing the velocity of the vehicle
    ☒ C decreasing the mass of the vehicle ✓
    ☐ D decreasing the time taken to change momentum

    (Total for Question 2 = 7 marks)

55   56   57   58

3. (a) A scientist is working in the countryside to investigate levels of radioactivity on a remote moor. A Geiger–Muller detector is used to measure the count rate. The level recorded is an average of 25 counts per minute.

    (i) Give the name of the radiation that the scientist is measuring.

    (1 mark)

    background radiation ✓

    (ii) State two sources of this radiation.

    (2 marks)

    radon gas ✓

    rocks ✓

    Alternative answers to 3(a)(ii): You could also state:
    - cosmic rays
    - nuclear industry

    (b) The scientist places a radioactive sample in front of the Geiger–Muller detector and takes some more measurements. The levels recorded now have an average of 200 corrected counts per minute.

    (i) Describe what the scientist does to determine the corrected count rate.

    (1 mark)

    He or she subtracts the mean background count rate from the measured count rate. ✓

    (ii) Explain why the scientist wears a photographic film badge while he carries out his research.

    (2 marks)

    In order to check how much radiation the scientist has been exposed to ✓ and make sure that he is safe. ✓

    Alternative answer to 4(b)(ii): You could also give:
    - To check that the scientist has not been exposed to too much radiation.

(c) Describe the nature of alpha, beta and gamma radiation in terms of ionising properties.

(3 marks)

Alpha radiation is highly ionising because the alpha particle is the most massive particle, so it can easily ionise atoms by knocking off their electrons. ✓

Beta radiation is moderately ionising because, although the particles are highly energised, they are very small, and so have less chance of knocking electrons off other atoms. ✓

Gamma radiation is the least ionising because it has no mass. ✓

(Total for Question 3 = 9 marks)

4. Figure 2 shows the graph of a radio wave.

Figure 2

(a) On the graph:

    (i) Identify the amplitude of the wave by adding 'A' next to an arrow or marker.

    (1 mark)

    (ii) Identify the time period of the wave by adding 'T' with arrows or markers.

    (1 mark)

    (iii) Determine the time period of the wave.

    (1 mark)

    $T = \dfrac{0.0001}{2}$

    $T = 0.00005s$ ✓

(b) Determine the frequency of the wave shown in the diagram.

(2 marks)

Period = 0.000 05 s

Frequency = 1 ÷ period

Frequency = 1 ÷ 0.000 05 s ✓

Frequency = 20 000 ✓ Hz

(c) Write the equation linking wave speed, wavelength and time period.

(1 mark)

wave speed = wavelength × time period ✓

(Total for Question 4 = 6 marks)

Alternative answers to 4(a)(i): You could also state:
- communications
- mobile phones

Alternative answers to 4(a)(ii): You could also state:
- security marking
- disinfecting water

Alternative answers to 4(a)(iii): You could also state:
- detecting cancer
- sterilising food or water

5. Figure 3 shows part of the electromagnetic spectrum.

Figure 3

(a) State one use for each of the following waves:

    (i) microwaves

    (1 mark)

    cooking ✓

    (ii) ultraviolet

    (1 mark)

    tanning ✓

    (iii) gamma rays

    (1 mark)

    treating cancer ✓

(b) Explain which of the waves in (a) is the most damaging to body cells.

(2 marks)

Gamma rays are the most damaging ✓ because they carry the most energy and are highly ionising. ✓

(c) Which one of the following terms best describes the nature of electromagnetic waves?

(1 mark)

- ☐ A longitudinal
- ☐ B mechanical
- ☐ C seismic
- ☒ D transverse ✓

(d) Light from the Sun takes 500 seconds to reach Earth, travelling at 3×10^8 m/s. Calculate the distance of Earth from the Sun. Give your answer in kilometres.

(3 marks)

speed = distance ÷ time
distance = speed × time
distance = 3×10^8 m/s × 500 s ✓
distance = 1.5×10^{11} m ✓

Distance = ...1.5×10^8..... ✓ km

(e) Explain why satellites are not used to transmit radio waves but are used to transmit microwaves.

(4 marks)

Satellites are not used to transmit radio waves because they are outside the Earth's atmosphere and radio waves cannot pass through the ionosphere. ✓ They are reflected back towards the Earth by the ionosphere. ✓ Satellites are used to transmit microwaves back to a receiving aerial on Earth from beams (using dish antennae) which are sent to a satellite, ✓ because microwaves can penetrate the ionosphere. ✓

(Total for Question 5 = 13 marks)

---

6. (a) A lift travels between floors in a building. The lift moves from the ground floor to the fourth floor through a height of 15 m in 20 s. The mass of the lift is 750 kg.

(i) Calculate how much energy, in joules (J), the lift gains in moving from the ground floor to the fourth floor. Take g to be 10 N/kg.

(2 marks)

ΔGPE = mass × g × change in height
ΔGPE = 750 kg × 10 N/kg × 15 m ✓

Energy gained, ΔGPE = ...112 500... ✓ J

(ii) Calculate the average power, in watts (W), that the lift exerts in moving the mass of 750 kg to the fourth floor.

(2 marks)

$Power = \dfrac{ΔGPE}{time\ taken}$

$Power = \dfrac{112\,500\ J}{20\ s}$ ✓

Power = ...5625... ✓ W

(b) As the lift moves upwards, not all the energy supplied is usefully transferred. Suggest one way in which energy is not usefully transferred.

(1 mark)

It is transferred to the thermal energy store of the motor. ✓

Alternative answers:
You could also suggest:
- thermal energy store of the elevator materials
- thermal energy store of the environment
- sound energy store

(c) Calculate the kinetic energy (KE), in J, of the lift when it is moving from the ground floor to the fourth floor.

(4 marks)

$Speed = \dfrac{distance\ travelled}{time\ taken}$

$Speed = \dfrac{15\ m}{20\ s}$ ✓

Speed = 0.75 m/s ✓

KE = ½ × mass × speed² = ½ × 750 kg × (0.75 m/s)² ✓

Kinetic energy = ...210.9... ✓ J

(d) Explain why this mechanical process could be described as wasteful.

Give an example of wasted energy in this process.

(3 marks)

This process could be described as wasteful because it causes a rise in temperature in parts of the system, ✓ and so transfers energy by heating the surroundings, which is not useful. ✓ An example is the rise in temperature of the lift motor. ✓

Alternative answers:
You could also suggest examples such as:
- rise in temperature of the fabric of the lift
- rise in temperature of the lift cables

(Total for Question 6 = 12 marks)
TOTAL FOR PAPER = 60

Combined Science
Paper 6: Physics 2

Time allowed: 1 hour 10 minutes

Answer ALL questions. Write your answers in the spaces provided.

1. (a) A kettle is rated at 2000 W and designed to operate on a 230 V mains supply. Calculate the charge moved in the kettle in 1 second.

(2 marks)

Power = 2000 W = 2000 J/s so energy in 1 second = 2000 J ✓

$E = Q \times V$
$Q = \dfrac{E}{V}$
$Q = \dfrac{2000}{230}$

Charge = ...8.7... ✓ C

(b) Explain what happens to the energy in various parts of the system when the kettle is switched on.

(3 marks)

Electrical energy is transferred to the thermal energy store of the kettle's heater. ✓ The kettle's heater then transfers energy to the thermal energy store of the water and the kettle jug. ✓ The water and the kettle transfer energy to the thermal energy store of the environment. ✓

(c) Draw an energy transfer diagram to illustrate the energy transferred inside the kettle after it has been switched on.

(3 marks)

(d) Describe how energy is not transferred usefully while boiling water in the kettle.

(2 marks)

Energy transferred as sound energy ✓ and in heating the material of the kettle ✓ is not useful.

Alternative answer:
You could also suggest:
• Energy is transferred to the environment.

(Total for Question 1 = 10 marks)

67

---

2. (a) The diagram in Figure 1 shows a wire passing through a card.

Figure 1

A compass is positioned at various places on the card to determine the direction of the magnetic field round the wire. Explain whether the magnetic field is clockwise or anticlockwise.

(3 marks)

The direction of the magnetic field will be clockwise ✓ as the current ✓ flows from positive to negative ✓.

(b) (i) The wire is now turned into a solenoid. Draw the new magnetic field that this produces.

(4 marks)

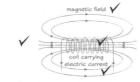

Diagram should be the correct shape, lines of flux very close inside, lines of flux further apart outside and pattern indicated on both sides of the electromagnet.

68

(ii) Suggest a use for this device.

(1 mark)

speaker ✓

(c) A 0.75 m length of wire carrying a current of 3 A is placed between two magnets at right angles to the field of 0.5 T. Calculate the force experienced by the wire. Give the unit.

(3 marks)

force = magnetic flux density × current × length of wire
force = 0.5 T × 3 A × 0.75 m ✓

Force = 1.1 ✓ N ✓

(Total for Question 2 = 11 marks)

Alternative answers to 2(b)(ii): You could also suggest:
• doorbell
• electromagnet

Alternative answer to 2(c):
Magnetic flux density can also be referred to as field strength.

69

---

3. An electrical heater supplies electrical energy to a copper block of mass 2000 g at 12 V with a current of 12 A for 2 minutes.

(a) Calculate the energy supplied to the heater. State the unit.

(3 marks)

energy supplied = current × potential difference × time
energy supplied = 12 A × 12 V × 120 s ✓

Energy supplied = 17 280 ✓ J ✓

(b) Calculate the temperature rise for the block of copper when supplied with the energy from (a) (your answer). The specific heat capacity of copper is 385 J/kg K. State the unit.

(3 marks)

$$\text{Change in temperature} = \frac{\text{change in heat energy}}{(\text{mass} \times \text{specific heat capacity})}$$

$$= \frac{17\,280\ \text{J}}{(2\ \text{kg} \times 385\ \text{J/kg K})} ✓$$

Temperature rise = 22.4 ✓ K or °C ✓

(c) Suggest why the actual temperature rise may be lower than the predicted value.

(1 mark)

Some of the thermal energy is dissipated to the environment. ✓

70

97

(d) (i) Give one way to reduce unwanted energy transfer in the heating of a metal block.

(1 mark)

You could thermally insulate the block. ✓

(ii) Give an example of a suitable material that could be used.

(1 mark)

cotton wool ✓

(Total for Question 3 = 9 marks)

71

---

4. Indoor skydivers use a vertical wind tunnel. Moving air travels upwards and keeps a skydiver at a constant height inside the tunnel.

(a) (i) Draw a labelled free body diagram to show the vertical forces acting on a skydiver hovering in a vertical wind tunnel.

(2 marks)

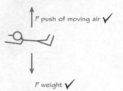

F push of moving air ✓

F weight ✓

(ii) When the wind tunnel is turned off, the skydiver moves towards the ground. Draw a labelled free body diagram to show the vertical forces acting on the skydiver as this happens.

(2 marks)

F air resistance ✓

F weight ✓

72

(b) The cyclist shown in Figure 2 is accelerating downhill on a bicycle by pushing on the pedals.

Figure 2

(i) Identify the force pairs acting on the cyclist and bicycle.

(2 marks)

Weight of rider and bicycle and the reaction force of ground on the bicycle ✓

Push of the cyclist and air resistance ✓

(ii) Sketch a labelled free body diagram to show how these forces are acting on the cyclist and bicycle.

(2 marks)

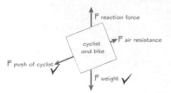

F reaction force

F air resistance

cyclist and bike

F push of cyclist ✓

F weight ✓

73

(c) Explain how the bicycle transfers energy to the surroundings. Suggest one way in which these transfers can be reduced.

(2 marks)

The moving parts of the bicycle transfer thermal energy to the environment due to friction. ✓ This can be reduced by lubricating them. ✓

(Total for Question 4 = 10 marks)

74

Figure 3 is a circuit diagram that shows three identical lamps and one cell.

Figure 3

(a) The cell provides 1.5 V. State the potential difference across each lamp.

(1 mark)

Each lamp would have a potential difference of 0.5 V across it. ✓

(b) Figure 4 shows a circuit to test a thermistor.

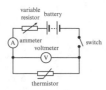

Figure 4

(i) Describe how resistance changes in a thermistor.

(3 marks)

When the temperature rises, ✓ the resistance falls, ✓ allowing more current to flow. ✓

(ii) Give a use for a thermistor in a domestic circuit.

(1 mark)

The thermostat in a central heating system ✓

> **Alternative answer to 5(b)(i):** You could also give the reverse answer:
>
> When the temperature falls, the resistance rises, allowing less current to flow.

> **Alternative answer to to 5(b)(ii):** You could also suggest:
> - any temperature-sensing circuit in the home, such as a toaster or electric kettle.

(c) Give a reason why the voltage of the electricity from the National Grid is reduced for domestic use, and state how this is done.

(2 marks)

The high voltages used in the National Grid are too dangerous for domestic use. ✓ A step-down transformer is used ✓ to reduce the voltage.

(d) (i) Calculate the current in the secondary coil of a step-down transformer, where $V_P = 4600$ V, $I_P = 5$ A and $V_s = 230$ V.

(2 marks)

$$V_P \times I_P = V_s \times I_s$$

$$I_s = \frac{V_P \times I_P}{V_s}$$

$$I_s = \frac{4600 \text{ V} \times 5 \text{ A}}{230 \text{ V}} \checkmark$$

Current = ...100 ✓........... A

(ii) State the assumption made when calculating the power of a transformer.

(1 mark)

We have assumed that the transformer is 100% efficient. ✓

(Total for Question 5 = 10 marks)

Two students carry out an experiment to investigate the linear elastic distortion of a thin spring. They add weights to a spring but can find only five weights: one of 0.1 N, one of 0.5 N and three of 1 N. They then measure the final extension. When the spring is unloaded the students find that the spring has stretched.

(a) Suggest two ways of improving the experiment.

(2 marks)

The students could add smaller weights each time ✓ and they should unload the spring after measuring each extension to check that the distortion is still elastic. ✓

> **Alternative answers:** You could also suggest:
> - finding different weights
> - extending the experiment by using a second variable – different size spring or different material.

(b) The table in Figure 5 shows results for the loading of a 32-mm spring.

Weight (N)	Length of spring (mm)
0	32
0.1	36
0.2	40
0.3	44
0.4	48
0.5	52
0.6	56

✓ ✓

Figure 5

Complete the missing values in the table.

(2 marks)

*(c) The students used their results to produce Figure 6. Explain how the graph illustrates linear elastic distortion and how the graph could be improved. Explain how you could extend the experiment to find out the force which makes the spring change shape permanently. You should refer to the graph in your answer.

(6 marks)

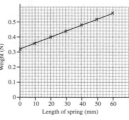

Figure 6

The graph shows that the length of the spring is proportional to the weight added (force) because it is a straight line. For every 0.1 N added the spring extends by 4 mm.

If the students had calculated the extension by subtracting the original length of the spring (32 mm) from the length of the spring after the weights had been added, that would have given the extension. The line would then have gone through the origin (0,0) and shown that the relationship between force and extension is directly proportional.

If the students added progressively more weight, the material might permanently change shape. The force would continue to increase but the extension would not increase as much as before. This would mean that the extended or extrapolated line on the graph would start to level off or curve towards the horizontal. The straight line should be labelled 'elastic region' and the curved line should be labelled 'inelastic region'. The point at which the straight line stopped should be labelled 'elastic limit'.

(Total for Question 6 = 10 marks)

TOTAL FOR PAPER = 60

The Periodic Table of the Elements

Key

1
H
hydrogen
1

relative atomic mass
atomic symbol
name
atomic (proton) number

1	2												3	4	5	6	7	0
1 **H** hydrogen 1																		4 **He** helium 2
7 **Li** lithium 3	9 **Be** beryllium 4												11 **B** boron 5	12 **C** carbon 6	14 **N** nitrogen 7	16 **O** oxygen 8	19 **F** fluorine 9	20 **Ne** neon 10
23 **Na** sodium 11	24 **Mg** magnesium 12												27 **Al** aluminium 13	28 **Si** silicon 14	31 **P** phosphorus 15	32 **S** sulfur 16	35.5 **Cl** chlorine 17	40 **Ar** argon 18
39 **K** potassium 19	40 **Ca** calcium 20	45 **Sc** scandium 21	48 **Ti** titanium 22	51 **V** vanadium 23	52 **Cr** chromium 24	55 **Mn** manganese 25	56 **Fe** iron 26	59 **Co** cobalt 27	59 **Ni** nickel 28	63.5 **Cu** copper 29	65 **Zn** zinc 30		70 **Ga** gallium 31	73 **Ge** germanium 32	75 **As** arsenic 33	79 **Se** selenium 34	80 **Br** bromine 35	84 **Kr** krypton 36
85 **Rb** rubidium 37	88 **Sr** strontium 38	89 **Y** yttrium 39	91 **Zr** zirconium 40	93 **Nb** niobium 41	96 **Mo** molybdenum 42	[98] **Tc** technetium 43	101 **Ru** ruthenium 44	103 **Rh** rhodium 45	106 **Pd** palladium 46	108 **Ag** silver 47	112 **Cd** cadmium 48		115 **In** indium 49	119 **Sn** tin 50	122 **Sb** antimony 51	128 **Te** tellurium 52	127 **I** iodine 53	131 **Xe** xenon 54
133 **Cs** caesium 55	137 **Ba** barium 56	139 **La*** lanthanum 57	178 **Hf** hafnium 72	181 **Ta** tantalum 73	184 **W** tungsten 74	186 **Re** rhenium 75	190 **Os** osmium 76	192 **Ir** iridium 77	195 **Pt** platinum 78	197 **Au** gold 79	201 **Hg** mercury 80		204 **Tl** thallium 81	207 **Pb** lead 82	209 **Bi** bismuth 83	[209] **Po** polonium 84	[210] **At** astatine 85	[222] **Rn** radon 86
[223] **Fr** francium 87	[226] **Ra** radium 88	[227] **Ac*** actinium 89	[261] **Rf** rutherfordium 104	[262] **Db** dubnium 105	[266] **Sg** seaborgium 106	[264] **Bh** bohrium 107	[277] **Hs** hassium 108	[268] **Mt** meitnerium 109	[271] **Ds** darmstadtium 110	[272] **Rg** roentgenium 111								

Elements with atomic numbers 112–116 have been reported but not fully authenticated

*The lanthanoids (atomic numbers 58–71) and the actinoids (atomic numbers 90–103) have been omitted.

100

Physics Equations List

(final velocity)^2 − (initial velocity)^2 = 2 × acceleration × distance $v^2 - u^2 = 2 \times a \times x$
force = change in momentum ÷ time $F = \dfrac{(mv - mu)}{t}$
energy transferred = current × potential difference × time $E = I \times V \times t$
force on a conductor at right angles to a magnetic field carrying a current = magnetic flux density × current × length $F = B \times I \times l$
potential difference across primary coil × current in primary coil = potential difference across secondary coil × current in secondary coil $V_p \times I_p = V_s \times I_s$
change in thermal energy = mass × specific heat capacity × change in temperature $\Delta Q = m \times c \times \Delta\theta$
thermal energy for a change of state = mass × specific latent heat $Q = m \times L$
energy transferred in stretching = 0.5 × spring constant × (extension)^2 $E = \frac{1}{2} \times k \times x^2$

Published by Pearson Education Limited, 80 Strand, London, WC2R 0RL.

www.pearsonschoolsandfecolleges.co.uk

Copies of official specifications for all Pearson qualifications may be found on the website: qualifications.pearson.com

Text and illustrations © Pearson Education Limited 2017
Typeset, illustrated and produced by Phoenix Photosetting
Cover illustration by Miriam Sturdee

The rights of Stephen Hoare, Nigel Saunders, Catherine Wilson, Allison Court and Alasdair Shaw to be identified as authors of this work have been asserted by them in accordance with the Copyright, Designs and Patents Act 1988.

First published 2017

20 19 18 17
10 9 8 7 6 5 4 3 2 1

British Library Cataloguing in Publication Data
A catalogue record for this book is available from the British Library

ISBN 978 1 292 21108 4

Printed in Slovakia by Neografia

Notes from the publisher
These Practice Papers are designed to complement your revision and to help prepare you for the exams. They do not include all the content and skills needed for the complete course and have been written to help you practise what you have learned. They may not be representative of a real exam paper. Remember that the official Pearson specification and associated assessment guidance materials are the only authoritative source of information and should always be referred to for definitive guidance.

Pearson has robust editorial processes, including answer and fact checks, to ensure the accuracy of the content in this publication, and every effort is made to ensure this publication is free of errors. We are, however, only human, and occasionally errors do occur. Pearson is not liable for any misunderstandings that arise as a result of errors in this publication, but it is our priority to ensure that the content is accurate. If you spot an error, please do contact us at resourcescorrections@pearson.com so we can make sure it is corrected.